Consider the Change

THE CHOICE IS YOURS

LEE M. SILVERSTEIN

Published by
Health Communications, Inc.
1721 Blount Road, Suite 1
Pompano Beach, Florida 33069

ISBN 0-932194-33-8

Printed in the United States of America

Cover Illustration and Design by Reta Kaufman
Photo by Chris Hewson

DEDICATED TO:

Sherrie Silverstein, who brings a unity of life with a deep and lasting love.

My children, Leslie, Jon, Amy, Debi and Elizabeth, who, each in their own way, have taught me much.

My family, Phyllis, Barbara, and Joan.

Jerry Edelwich, Smokey Orcutt, and John Woods, who are always there with unquestioning love.

Sid Simon, a constant source of personal and professional energy.

The support and care of Joan Curry.

And I miss: Don Flannagan, dogged by the past, dogged by pain. I pray he has finally achieved peace.

Harry Chapin, whose words continue to move me.

iii

THANKS TO:

Gary Seidler and Peter Vegso of Health Communications, Inc., for their support and faith over the years.

The people of Greece, who have adopted me in the way my own self-help program has.

The community at Wernersville, PA, that allowed the process to take place again.

Carole Sturgis, Frank Vogel, Claire Kusmick, who were there when this project started, and Jackie Weaver, who helped tie up the threads at the end.

Brenda Wright and Valerie Murphy, for their extraordinary typing bouts. No praise is enough for their struggling with my handwriting as those who know will testify to.

Dan Bartmettler, who was the first person to bring my work to a national audience.

And Frank Horan, Claire Collins, Pat Kinnane, Bill Moriarty, David Powell, Charlie Pilkington and Dean Billingham.

AND . . . Muriel, Bonnie, Nicole, Marcie, Gary, Gus, Lois, Judy, Ginny, Tina, Sherry, John, Joan, Nick, Camille, Howard, Sandra, Mary, Arnie, Karen, Bunkie, Sandi, Lou, Wally, Jim, Connie, Norm, Betty, Jim, John, Nora, Sue, Gary, Dave, Don, Sissy, Len, Edith, Joe, Matt, Chuck, Charlie, Anne, George, Joe, Margarita, Max, LeClair, Charly, Walter, Issac, Wilma, Corky, Marie, Rene, Carrie, Pru, Gus, Lois, Dutch, Ocho, Linda, Michele, Judy, Margarita, Klaus, Karen, Costa . . . Joyce.

WELCOME

"The good fortune of my life is that I have met, loved (and disappointed) only exceptional human beings."

A. Camus

"The brontosaurus became extinct but it wasn't its fault, so to speak. If we become extinct it **will** be our fault. In order to survive, man has to evolve."

Dr. Jonas Salk

THE MEANING OF SIMPLICITY
"I hide behind simple things so you'll
find me;
If you don't find me, you'll find
the things,
You'll touch what my hand
has touched,
Our hand-prints will merge.
The August moon glitters in the
kitchen like a tin-plated pot (it gets
that way because of what I'm saying
to you),
It lights up the empty house and the
house's kneeling silence—
Always the silence remains kneeling.
Every word is a doorway
To a meeting, one often cancelled,
And that's when a word is true:
When it insists on the meeting."

Yannis Ritsos

"Weren't You Lee Silverstein?"

I stood alone in the dark, feeling hopeless, helpless, empty, sad. My life, at the moment, was unmanageable. It was my second night at a drug and alcohol rehabilitation center in Wernersville, PA, and I wanted to run away, but, to tell the truth, I wasn't even sure where Wernersville was.

Everything should have been wonderful. I was retired, living in Greece with my new wife, and planning to buy a villa on an island in the Aegean. But instead, I was here. Lee Silverstein, 16 years sober, author, lecturer, and therapist on the subject, now a resident at a treatment center. A doctor had prescribed sleeping pills following my heart attack and surgery. Despite my "knowing better," I opted to go along. In a few weeks I had started to abuse them. I was heading for trouble.

That night I felt unworthy of trust, inadequate, alienated, helpless. I felt so very "wrong" and in need of punishment for what I had done. I felt resentment, anger, and self-pity, which is my true disease, my true problem. For a moment, for the first time in 16 years, I felt life was not worthwhile.

Somehow I had lost my way. "Looking good but feeling bad." Fear from my near death heart attack, living with memories of oxygen tubes, not knowing if I would see morning and hold my family again, discouragement from my second heart operation, working at a new marriage, some of my children in crisis with serious physical and emotional problems, one of my best friends committing suicide, unresolved feelings about the death of my first wife, residual issues as an adult child of an alcoholic, guilt, and the sudden stop of retirement — watching the announcement of workshops, missing the "road," no longer able to divert, to run.

There were signs. Needing, demanding expectations to be met by others. A fear of unpredictable events (anxiety over death). I withdrew, was touchy and irritable. I was relying more and more on other people as to how I felt about myself.

I had forgotten that, when I put all of myself out to others, I need to have something coming in. I forgot that I don't function well when I hurt, that I make mistakes in living when I'm in pain, and I don't deal with the pain.

At times, I passed over the present in a race for the future. At times I found myself submerged, not by distractions, but by opportunities; not just by dull people, but by too many interesting people. Racing again. And within, noise instead of stillness.

Sixteen years sober but I had never really learned the meaning of sobriety. Still trying to please people. Still the little child begging for love. Always the oddball. Always looking to fit in. Still motivated by phantoms of guilt, shame. Slipping back into old tapes like Claudia Black's theme: Don't feel, don't talk, don't trust.

Run, run, run, like the gingerbread man, catch the real Lee Silverstein if you can.

Yes, I progressed in those 16 years, but I still wanted relief too fast, never wanted to feel inadequate.

I had avoided BEING by DOING.

The first four days at the treatment center I wept, alone. Everything I had written of, spoken of, lived, seemed empty and lost.

I had forgotten tragedy and pain can catch us all unguarded, that hurt, guilt, can lead to powerlessness

and unmanageability for us all.
Like Dory Previn's song: "*On My Way to Where?*"

> i
> how did i get this way
> i was
> what was i going to say
> i was on
> how did i get in here
> i was on my
> wasn't i here last year
> i was on my way
> why have they put me in
> i was on my way to
> who is my next of kin
> won't i ever win
> i paid
> my airplane fare
> i was
> on my way to where . . .

I had forgotten that I have choices, good choices, at all times.

Basically, I needed to be re-educated in faith, trust, love. I had slipped back into resentments, anger, self pity. Self pity. I had paid my dues. I had handled so much for so long, so well. Why now? Why me? Why not? So much for perfection. Welcome back to the human race.

I was, as Kris Kristofferson sings: "A walking contradiction, partly truth and partly fiction." I found I, too, am prey to error and weakness, and to the pain that never sleeps, the pain that must eventually be answered by all of us, whenever, wherever.

So, like my clients, I had to look and ask myself:
Where am I at? What am I doing to me?
What is not working as well as I want it to?
What do I really, really, really want?
What consequences do I face?
What inconsistencies need to be dealt with?
What will make my life better?

What alternatives do I have?
Have I considered those alternatives?

I chose to ask for help despite being embarrassed, angry, guilty ("I should know better, do better"). I started to relearn to trust the process. I started to relearn my values, tools, skills, my "program."

At times, visitors to the treatment center came up and told me how much my workshops based on my book, *"Consider the Alternative,"* helped them. Someone else stopped to ask me, "Weren't you Lee Silverstein who wrote that book?" O Lord, the shame I felt in those first few days, and the fear of public exposure: "Look, that is who he really is, we always knew that."

One lesson I quickly relearned: admit, accept, and move on. Let people and the process work. Self-forgiveness is essential, yet it may be the hardest. Forgetting is not forgiving the condemnation that comes from within.

I relearned some of the ideas this book will discuss, how to create change and how to teach people they have the ability to change. The most important thing I learned was that my thinking can quickly go astray.

Today, most days, my life has never been better. I am happy. Most important I understand that I am happy. I am happy in being and knowing, in spite of and because of events and circumstances. I know that I am in charge of my choices and in charge of my life.

Through reflection and guidance by the loving, caring staff members at the treatment center who were willing to accept me as just another resident, with the love and support of my special wife, special children, and special friends, along with tough scary work on my part, I did exactly what I have helped others do. I relearned that the process works, if I work the process and trust it unconditionally, that is, nothing less than 100 percent commitment. If I let go of people, places, things, need for approval, need to be loved, stuffed frozen feelings, fear of rejection, the process works.

I relearned to breathe out ego and to breathe in a

power greater than myself. I relearned gratitude for how much that higher power loved me to allow me to relearn.

And death is no longer such a fear. I can't hold up time, therefore I must make the most of each day.

Lessons - Lessons - Lessons

I can't make it all go way for anyone.

* * * *

Feeling less than OK keeps me from loving you.

* * * *

If I feel ugly I can only regain my humanness through another's love.

* * * *

My worst opponent is Me!

* * * *

"The Road to Holiness passes necessarily through the world of action."

—Dag Hammarskjold

* * * *

Going beyond the fear gives me an openness to life and beyond that to love.

* * * *

*If I **act** in good faith miracles appear and occur.*

* * * *

I detach from the past, from past injustices, and live in the present to forgive myself.

* * * *

I will be judged by the love I give.

* * * *

When I gain peace of mind, balance of mind, and humility, and forget the meaningless honors and acts, the impasses disappear.

* * * *

*"It's the heart afraid of breaking that never learns to dance.
It's the dream afraid of waking that never takes the chance.
It's the one who won't be taken who cannot seem to give.
And the soul afraid of dying that never learns to live."*

—The Rose

one

Trying to Control

Join me now as I look at the process with you. The goal is not an absence of fear or pain, not that I will handle everything or that I will be free of problems, but that I will come to an awareness that I can work through the pain. I don't have the answer, I only search. I hope you decide to become a searcher with me.

One of my gurus, James Kavanaugh, put it this way in the introduction to his fine book *"Too Gentle to Live Among the Wolves:"*

> *"This is a book born in my heart, born in the pain of ending one life and beginning another, born in the excitement of the continuing search for life's meaning. Some people do not have to search, they find their niche early in life and rest there, seemingly contented and resigned. They do not seem to take it seriously. At times I envy them, but usually I do not understand them. Seldom do they understand me.*
>
> *I am one of the searchers. There are, I believe, millions of us. We are not unhappy, but neither are we really content. We continue to explore life, hoping to uncover its ultimate secret. We continue to explore ourselves, hoping to understand. We like to walk along the beach, we are drawn by the ocean, taken by its power, its unceasing motion, its mystery and unspeakable beauty. We like forests and mountains, deserts and hidden rivers, and the lonely cities as well. Our sadness is as much a part of our lives as is our laughter. To share our sadness with one we love is perhaps as great a joy as we can know—unless it be to share our laughter.*
>
> *We searchers are ambitious only for life itself, for everything beautiful it can provide. Most of all we want to love and be loved. We want to live in a relationship that will not impede our wandering, nor prevent our search, nor lock us in prison walls; that will take us for what little we have to give. We do not want to prove*

ourselves to another or to compete for love.

This book is for wanderers, dreamers and lovers, for lonely men and women who dare to ask of life every-thing good and beautiful. It is for those who are too gentle to live among wolves."

I also ask that you keep everything in life in perspective. Someone sent me an anonymous copy of a letter they had received from their daughter, who was away at college. It went:

Dear Mother and Dad:

Since I left for college, I have been remiss in writing and I am sorry for my thoughtlessness in not having written before. I will bring you up to date now, but before you read on, please sit down. You are not to read any further unless you are sitting down. Okay?

Well, then, I am getting along pretty well now. The skull fracture and the concussion I got when I jumped out of the window of my dormitory when it caught fire shortly after my arrival here is pretty well healed by now. I only spent two weeks in the hospital and now I can see almost normally and only get those sick head-aches once a day. Fortunately, the fire in the dormitory, and my jump, was witnessed by an attendant at the gas station near the dorm, and he was the one who called the Fire Department and the ambulance. He also visited me in the hospital and since I had nowhere to live because of the burnt-out dormitory, he was kind enough to invite me to share his apartment with him. It's really a basement room, but it's kind of cute. He is a very fine boy and we have fallen deeply in love and are planning on getting married. We haven't set the exact date yet, but it will be before my pregnancy begins to show.

Yes, Mother and Dad, I am pregnant. I know how much you are looking forward to being grandparents and I know you will welcome the baby and give it the same love and devotion and tender care you gave me when I was a child. The reason for the delay in our marriage is that my boy friend has a minor infection

2

which prevents us from passing our pre-marital blood tests and I carelessly caught it from him.

I know that you will welcome him into our family with open arms. He is kind, and although not well educated, he is ambitious. Although he is of a different race and religion than ours, I know your often-expressed tolerance will not permit you to be bothered by that.

Now that I have brought you up to date, I want to tell you that there was no dormitory fire; I did not have a concussion or skull fracture; I was not in the hospital; I am not pregnant; I am not engaged; I am not infected, and there is no boy friend in my life. However, I am getting a "D" in History, and an "F" in Science, and I want you to see these marks in their proper perspective.

—Your loving daughter

We live in a crazy, insane, bizarre world. Even here in Greece, a really special talented humanistic psychologist whom I've had the privilege of sharing with, Charis Katakis, has developed much work on the concept of "entropy," which speaks of the disorder, conflict and human suffering we all go through. Some professionals, like R. D. Laing, believe our world is so crazy that many people remove themselves mentally to protect themselves from the bombardment of insanity we face from all areas of living. Some people "burn out" like the concept my friend Jerry Edelwich pioneered about in his book, *Burnout*. Some choose to "crack-up" like the Glasserians believe. Some "rust out" by choosing Systematic Suicide, which I first learned of from Sid Simon, and will discuss some of my thoughts on that in a later chapter. Some, like Albert Ellis, believe it is not the world or events that cause this, because events are neutral — it is our thoughts about the events that create our anger, depression, violence.

* * *

What are we bombarded with?
On TV: Just a week's sampling of "life"

3

ALL MY CHILDREN

Sybil threw a tantrum when Cliff and Nina reconciled. Devon agreed to join A.A. so that Wally won't take Bonnie away. Joe kissed away Leora's tears over Curt. Aunt Clara advised Ruth to save her marriage by getting over her neurosis about Joey. Tad stole cookie-jar money from Kate to support his drug habit. Peg grew ill and Brooke learned that Ed died nearly bankrupt. Palmer and Donna's ski trip was shortened because of her shoulder injury. Myrtle blackmailed Langley to rehire Benny. Devon was on a bender but a car screeched when Bonnie ran into the street. Sean implied to Palmer that Sean has the "inside track" with Nina.

ANOTHER WORLD

Zachary transferred Jamie to Ogden prison before Rachel and Mac returned with Mitch. Sandy didn't "turn a trick" with Tracy, who became a pal, then revealed that Mac is his father. Marianne asked Rick for time before she's capable of returning his love declarations. Jason denied that he consented to Ilsa setting up Tracy and Sandy. Ilsa assumed she'd be doing a favor for Jason by planting a bomb in Russ' car. Ada agreed to use Charlie's insurance money to open the beauty parlor, with Clarice as assistant. Larry accepted dough from Jordon. Olivia convinced Pat and Philip to work in emergency care. Rachel didn't tell Mitch the whole truth about their past.

AS THE WORLD TURNS

Margo was devastated by Lyla's confession that John is Margo's daddy. Margo cried on James' shoulder, then fell into his bed. James and Eric told Hayley that her father died. John helped Hayley through the crisis, but she didn't believe it was an accidental death. Lyla returned Bob's engagement ring. Tom and Maggie clashed over trial tactics. She demolished David's testimony, then called Dee as a defense witness. Steve insisted that he and Andrea resume their affair now that Nick knows the score. Margo refused to accept Lyla's excuses about John, who doesn't want a daughter like Margo any more than she wants John as a dad. Kim urged Steve to tell Carol the truth about Andrea.

In newspapers and magazines here is a sampling of stories:

- In Long Island, New York, a 36-year-old Veteran who was denied help at a local VA hospital after saying he feared he might do harm to himself or others went home and beat his mother to death with a hammer.

- A 17-year-old pregnant woman in Beaumont, Texas, was forced to give birth at home without professional care because a local hospital refused help when she appeared (in labor), because she had had her prenatal care in another hospital one hour away.

- A Virginia Beach man's mother-in-law died after he hit her with a hatchet 18 times. He told police he mistook her for a raccoon.

- After John Belushi's sad, premature death—Dan Aykroyd gave a eulogy that said: "Real Greatness gives real license for great indulgence. There had to be an illicit thrill to make it all worthwhile." (So any of us who feel we are "Great" get a legitimate "license").

- John Hinckley's father told the court, "I am the cause of John's tragedy." (What is **the answer** to adequate parenting?)

- In Denver, a 14-year-old boy sued and won in small claims courts, a 45-cent award because one of his subscribers had tried to avoid paying him — after repeated attempts to collect.

- A new civil rights group — Gypsies Against Stereotypical Propaganda—was formed to prevent "slurs" against reading of palms, tarot cards and horoscopes.

- A prestigious hospital in New York City discharged an 81-year-old man who died two days later, by the side of his helpless, senile wife. The hospital did the discharge despite apparent knowledge there was not adequate care for the man at home. The doctor who did the discharge did so despite pleas from the hospital's social worker who knew the situation at home.

- In Dallas, a 21-year-old woman was doused with

5

gasoline and set on fire during an argument with her ex-boyfriend.

- Washington, D.C. has a National Condom Week. Recently, in conjunction with this, the National Condom Week Task Force held its Fourth Annual Rubber Disco Dance. As a highlight to the dance the winner of a condom blowing contest received a $35 prize.

- A 200 lb. Cambridge, Mass. man was freed on $100 bond after being accused of raping a 21-month-old girl.

- In Lee County, Florida, a man got the "Armed Citizen Award" for killing with one bullet from his .357 Magnum an alleged robber. The award was for "his act of citizenship."

- New York State changed their rape law so that victims must **prove** to "have fear of immediate death or serious physical injury."

- Four million Massachusetts auto inspection stickers wouldn't stick.

- A Queens couple was taken in handcuffs to State Police Headquarters during a "vacation" in the Catskill Mountains because the motel they were staying in felt $13 worth of towels were ruined with make-up. "I'm really afraid to use towels now when I travel. When we go out to dinner, I'm afraid to use the napkins. I laugh now, but it was frightening when it happened," the lady involved said.

- A mayor in New Britain, Connecticut was in trouble with a local union, when he tried to clean a weed-choked Vietnam War Memorial one Saturday afternoon. One hundred veterans from 27 different Veterans organizations, the union local, and the State of Connecticut Board of Labor Relations were involved and probably could have built a new memorial for the costs involved.

- In Louisiana an undertaker got in trouble for cutting the legs and arms from a body so the corpse could fit in a smaller casket.

- In Boston a convicted murderer filed a malpractice suit against a psychiatric hospital for releasing him before he went out to commit the murder.

- In Chicago a parapalegic was denied permission to marry in a church because he could not "consummate" the marriage.

- The NFL a few seasons ago fined a team $1,000 because some of the players wore their socks too low thus allowing some bare leg to show.

- The University of Colorado has a new concern group—funded at $7,000 a year—The "Orgasm Concern Group."

- The search for high-tech sexual pleasure goes on with the search (not for the grail) but for the G. Spot. Does a best seller on this indicate whether the Grafenberg Spot is there, or how many people want to search for it? Between Kinsey's statistics and Masters & Johnsons' vibrators, there seems to be a masturbatory conspiracy to keep men and women from finding and enjoying themselves in bed. Salvation through orgasm. It seems at times that any climax reached in less than three hours will be considered premature.

- In Columbus, Ohio, a body was left hanging in a cell for over one hour while shifts changed. "Due to restrictions on overtime, detectives had to change shifts in the middle of the investigation."

- A 4-year-old in California died because the mother failed to have a Medi-Cal card when she tried to get him into the hospital. The boy died shortly after of spinal meningitis. According to reports, "The hospital policy was no money, no Blue Cross, no credit card, no entrance."

- In Maryland, a rape charge was dropped from first to second degree. The victim, a 33-year-old mother of three, testified she was grabbed from behind, slapped in the face, dragged into the woods, had her clothes ripped off and was raped. The court ruled she did not prove Fear of Serious Physical Injury (defined as death, suffocation, strangulation, disfigurement).

As a final note in some of the "craziness" of our world—

MARK BODY BEFORE SURGERY, SPECIALISTS ADVISE
SACRAMENTO, Calif. (UPI) — Edgy patients going under the scalpel may want to leave a note on their bodies reminding surgeons which part to slice.

That's the advice of two medical specialists disturbed by newspaper accounts of a child whose healthy eye was mistakenly removed in surgery.

In a letter recently published in the Journal of the American Medical Association, Dr. Harvey Cain and surgical assistant Janet Peyton, both of Kaiser Hospital, advised that the words, "Not on this side," should be inked with a pen onto the healthy side of a patient about to undergo surgery.

A clear plastic tag could be substituted for "people who don't like to be written on," Ms. Peyton said. She and the doctor suggested that the cautious patient even initial the warning to allay fears that a surgeon will remove the wrong leg, eye, breast, or kidney.

The article goes on to show how this can prevent a lot of "litigation"—not to mention heartache.

Read "Ann Landers" or "Dear Abby."

"REMEDY MAY BE WORSE THAN KNUCKLE-BITING"
DEAR ANN: My husband has a serious psychological problem. He bites his knuckles constantly. It has bothered me throughout the 15 years we've been married.

One day last week I saw him doing it, and I just got fed up. So I went over and slapped his glasses off. He slapped me back, which made me angry because I only slapped him for his own good. So I slapped him again. He then pounced on me with his fist. To make him stop, I kicked him in the shin. Well, it turns out I broke his leg.

My husband is home from the hospital now with a cast on and I've been going to a psychiatrist. I'm determined to get him to stop that childish habit. Whenever I see him biting his knuckles, I kick his cast. It seems to be working because he is biting his knuckles less.

I realize my husband is using his temporary handicap to manipulate me into seeking therapy, and I resent it.

Actually, He is the one who should be seeing a shrink. May I have your candid opinion? — FRAMED AND RESENTFUL.

DEAR F. AND R. "*If you are kicking your husband in the cast after breaking his leg, I'd say you have a long way to go before you are qualified to decide who else needs therapy.*

Until you learn to rechannel your anger, Buttercup, you'd better keep your suggestions to yourself."

Listen to Country Western Music Titles like:

"*I'd Rather Have a Bottle in Front of Me Than a Frontal Lobotomy.*"
"*Flushed From the Bathroom of Your Heart.*"
"*She's Just a Name Dropper, and Now She's Droppin' Mine.*"
"*Thank God and Greyhound You're Gone.*"
"*Don't Tell Me You're Sorry. I Know How Sorry You Are.*"
"*If You Want to Keep the Beer Real Cold, Put It Next to My Ex's Heart.*"
"*From the Gutter to You is Not Up.*"

Ever try to get a computer to correct your credit card account?

Ever try to rent a car for cash, not a credit card?

Jack Newfield of the CBS Radio Network on the program, "Spectrum" on January 9, 1980 said it so well then and I believe it is true today:

"*There is something cheap, something rotten in our mass culture. Our values have become warped. Cocaine and over-priced designer jeans have become cultural icons. Last month, New York Magazine published an unhealthy obsession with gossip. What America needs is a **real** moral majority.*

The best-seller lists are filled with how-to books— not books that tell you how to love and feel, but how to enjoy quick, disposable sex. The best-seller lists also have books that teach us how to intimidate and manipulate other people, and how to get rich quick without

9

doing any hard work. There are no best-selling books on sharing, or kindness, or on the shallowness of materialism. Television is dominated by car chases, dull sit-coms, and trash sports. Every Saturday morning there are violent cartoons for the kids. On TV, women, blacks and gays are usually stereotypes. Television has become bubble gum for the eyes.

Our politicians have become celebrities with pretty faces: Kemp the football star, Glenn the astronaut, Reagan the actor, Bradley the basketball player. I have a fantasy that the country will not have an election. Jack Kemp and Bill Bradley will just compete in a trash sports battle of the network stars, and the winner of the kayak race will become President.

Who are our heroes? A top star singer pals around with gangsters. A "champion" fighter quits in the middle of a fight for which he was paid $8 million to give his best. Most of our pop stars take drugs. One of our most influential folk-pop songwriters is accused of beating up his wife. Who can the next generation look up to?

The answer is there are quiet heroes and wise men of the tribe, modestly working away. But **People** *magazine and the TV programmers don't care about quality because they think it is boring. Saul Bellow and Bernard Malamud still write their novels. The books of Rebecca West and V. S. Pritchett can still be found in libraries. There are good teachers, and good cops, and good carpenters.*

A culture that doesn't appreciate values like wisdom, discipline, a sense of history and hard work is in a lot of trouble."

I, like Albert Ellis, believe I get stuck not because of what is happening to me, but because I believe it "should," "ought to," "must" be different. At times I decide what should be and try to control the people and things around me.

In the past I tried to exert control with drugs and alcohol. Others may use tranquilizers, antidepressants, smoking, food, psycho-therapy, relaxation techniques, meditation, cults, biofeedback, hypnosis, diets, vitamins, on and on.

Today I try to control in other ways. When my wife and I moved to Greece, I decided her transition to Greece should be a satisfactory, happy experience. I tried to make her happy. I gave up friends, tried always to be available to her. At times she felt helpless, then she would get angry with me for rescuing her, and I would get depressed because I couldn't satisfy her, and round and round it went. As my friend, John Woods, says: "Walking on egg shells hurts."

In the end, I lost friends, failed to make my wife happy, and was miserable. My choice — my responsibility — my "craziness."

When I suffered my heart attack, I felt and reacted like I was a time bomb, instead of realizing that the more I stressed myself with concern, depression, and anger, the worse my heart would be.

Everyone seeks answers to the conflict and confusion that cause pain in their lives. I, like everyone, want a life that makes sense and gives me a feeling of well being. So, I look for people to care for me. I look to impress others, manipulate others, in order to be safe, to be loved.

This drive for belonging sends us all on a search for the good parent, for justice, for acceptance, and yet we so often feel let down, exploited, betrayed, or rejected.

Starting as a child, I tried every way known to get some clear sign of approval, of reassurance, from my parents. I stuffed my feelings, I never spoke back. Today, I know I just had to be me, whatever that was, and accept me and let them handle their own problems and feelings.

The Problem Areas Mount:

- physical
- substance abuse
- financial
- organizational
- situational
- marital
- sexual
- anxiety
- stress
- depression
- sadness
- adjustment
- separation

- medical
- legal
- work
- dissatisfaction
- family
- children
- emotional

- frustration
- anger
- grief
- loss
- divorce
- identity

These problems invade all areas of our lives:

- family
- friendship
- morals
- religion
- financial
- school
- love
- creativity
- having fun
- health

- self
- society
- ethics
- leisure
- work
- relationship
- sexuality
- spontaneity
- future

The Conflicts Mount:

Work vs. Leisure

I struggle with this all the time. As Rainer Marie Rilke said: "For somewhere reigns an old hostility between our living and our great work."

And Yeats: "The intellect of man is forced to choose perfection of the life, or of the work, and if it takes the second, most refuse a heavenly mansion, raging in the dark."

Other conflicts:

Time with friends . . . time with family

Desire for intimacy . . . need for space, autonomy

My needs . . . your needs

What do I believe about sexism?

racism?

poverty?

politics?

spiritual life?

my health?

my aging?

my death?

A typical day in my life, and maybe yours. My wife would like to redecorate our villa. We are short of cash and she doesn't want me to work too hard because of my health. Our children want money to meet some of their objectives. At the same time money is short. My wife feels I should more aggressively collect money others owe us. I owe others money. The banks are on strike and I can't pay the money. The local government wants me to get Greek license plates this week, but the banks are closed so I can't pay the license fees. The Air Force wants me to be available to do a seminar, but keeps postponing a date which prevents me from taking other work.

Delusion . . . acceptance.

I pretend not to know what I do know. I get into trouble with money this way by never saying "no" to my family. I delude myself that the pot will never run dry.

Control . . . freedom.

I want more of life but sometimes fear the freedom I have chosen in terms of freelance work, where I live, etc. I want freedom to fulfill my needs and to allow others to fulfill their needs, but I sometimes enforce my parental role.

Frozen feelings . . . sharing.

I still have a problem allowing others to share my fears with me. I can only cry and be vulnerable when alone.

Distance . . . closeness.

I want the closeness of love but fear the hurt of love, the possible abandonment.

Isolation . . . need
Power . . . ineffectiveness
Powerlessness . . . hope
Dependency . . . independence
Nothingness . . . identity
Trust . . . mistrust
Male . . . female

I want to let go, but I am terrified of the possible consequences. Trouble for my children, my work in disfavor, my friends not liking my choices.

1. List areas of conflict and confusion in your life . . . prioritize them.
2. Prioritize and specify how you deal with the three key areas, i.e. problem solving, getting along with other people, entertaining yourself.
3. What I suggest now is that you take a sheet of paper and reflect on what you've read in this chapter and the insights you've gained from the exercises above by using Sid Simon's Discovery Statements:

I learned that _____

_____

_____

I rediscovered _____

_____

_____

I'm beginning to wonder _____

_____

_____

I was surprised to find that _____

_____

_____

I would like to explore _____

_____

_____

Now, that I think of it, I _____

_____

_____

I would like to follow up on _____

_____

_____

I would like to make a contract with myself to __

_____

_____

I see the need to ask the support of _____

_____

_____

I want to think more about _____

_____

_____

two

How We Choose to Live

Health specialists say that 60% of illnesses are related to lifestyle. Lifestyle is the unique pattern of my daily life. It is the food I eat, a balanced diet or overeating. Lifestyle is the car I drive and the seatbelts I do or don't use. It's speeding or taking it easy. It's the alcohol I drink, the deadly one more for the road. It's moderation or alcoholism. It's knowing when to get treatment and getting it.

Lifestyle is the drugs I take, the cigarettes I smoke. It's abuse of over the counter drugs, use of illegal drugs, or intelligent use of medication.

Lifestyle is staying in shape or going to seed. It's participating in sports or being an observer. It's pursuing a hobby or sitting for hours watching television. It's getting out and doing something enjoyable or being bored.

Lifestyle is how I handle stress, tension and loneliness. It's knowing how to relax. It's how I feel about myself, my life, job, family, and friends. It's being able to change some things in my life and living with those I can't. It's contentment or despair.

My lifestyle, at this moment, whether good or bad, is distinctly my own. It will change according to my attitude and ability to change. My lifestyle reflects with reasonable accuracy what my health may be in the future, unless changes are made for the better.

I am what I eat, drink, breathe, think and do. What I become tomorrow depends on today.

It is also prevention. I can decrease my susceptibilty to the seven major known causes of death—cancer, automobile accidents, suicide, heart disease, chronic overindulgence and abuse of drugs, alcohol, food, violence and chronic stress. As a matter of fact, many cancer experts are seeing a relationship between stress and cancer, especially after a traumatic event, like the loss of an important relationship through death or other causes.

I applaud Dr. Bill Glasser's approach in his recent book, "Take Effective Control of Your Life," when he urges us to stop using "inaccurate noun forms" and change "headache" to "headaching" and "depression" to "depressing" and then goes into the whole area of suspected psychosomatic illnesses, which may be up to 85% of our illnesses, such as coronary heart disease, arthritis, eczema, ileitis, colitis, ulcers.

Glasser seems to believe that almost everything we do we choose to do. Thus, we are depressing, stressing, headaching, upsetting. My actions are total behaviors. I am responsible for my feelings in any situation. Likewise, I can choose differently. I have control over what I do which in turn affects what I think and feel.

For example, when I came to Greece I was advised to bring a car. It was very poor advice. Having a car in Greece meant mounds of paperwork. I depressed over it, angered over it, angered at the person who advised me. Then I decided I would get rid of the car, but this would mean much more money lost. Finally, after briefly wallowing in the depression and anger, I looked at what else I could do. I checked the so-called impossible situations and found a way to keep my car. No more paperwork. I acted and it cured my paralysis.

Death may not be the will of a Higher Power.
Death may not be chance.
Death may not be genes.
Death may not be luck.
Death may not be meant to be.

My death may be directly tied into how I choose to live, and that's a continuous process. A former patient, now close friend, whom I love dearly, wrote me:

"Dear Lee,
Hugh Beaumont died. I read that in the paper the other day without realizing what was significant about it to me. Later I remembered how I used to sit and watch

18

"Leave It To Beaver" and drink white port wine. I'd always be maudlin by the end. My face and I would both be stiff from tears and wine.

Funny the things that can keep you company. Billy once told me for him it was "Love of Life."

He hasn't called, by the way.

How do you do it? How do you deal with your friends when you've known them for so long . . . ?

I try to be objective. But it gets to me when they try to "B.S." me. It seems like such an affront. And then I think of how many times I've done the same thing; and how many times the person I thought I was conning must have been aware of it and let it go by. Just as I do now.

What a crazy disease!

A few weeks ago I was in a small spate of depression. What I like to do when that happens is get in the car and go for a ride by myself. I think I enjoy the confinement of the car (it's like a cell) coupled with the freedom of movement and travel.

A lot of times I just go down the Silas Deane Highway until I get to the end of Cromwell. Just before it turns into Route Nine, I turn around and come back.

It's a nice ride. Not too long or too short. When I was a kid I used to do it on a bike. There used to be an old abandoned quarry out there that had filled in with water and we used it as a swimming hole.

Maybe that's why I still drive out that way. It puts me in touch with a time that seems innocent from here.

We had to go to the quarry, and the water was kind of murky. But it was leafy and green and there was a rope that hung from a tree that we could swing out and drop into the water from. There was never anyone else there.

It's not there anymore. I heard they filled it in some time ago. Probably condominiums now.

There's a bar in Cromwell, too, that I used to go in later when I "grew up." I think Billy is the one who turned me on to it. Nice little hideaway in which to meet other men's wives. It used to be called "Wall Street."

It has had a lot of different names from then to

now—Dry Dock Tavern, and Newport News to name two—but as I drove past it this last time I noticed (I always look) the name was again "Wall Street." It was like some kind of signal.

I began to think I should stop and go in to see if it was the same inside. I could order a Coke, I thought.

Then I began to think, why a Coke? Why not a beer? Surely by now I could get away with one beer. I mean, after all these years, all the health and strength I've built, it couldn't lead to anything.

My God! What a disease! Just when you know you've got the beast whipped it raises its ugly head. The first sign of depression or sentimentality, the first hint of success or celebration, like a dozing dog sniffing a bitch in heat, up it jumps, alert, ready.

It's really such an easy disease to beat. Just stop drinking. It's the longevity of the cure that gets tricky.

How do you get something like that across to a friend? That it's not easy, but it's not hard either. That you actually can live without it, really live. All you can do with it is die.

And maybe that's why I sat down to write this.

The last time I talked to Billy, he didn't say it, but he sounded like he felt the way I used to feel when I used to sit sipping white port and watching "Leave It To Beaver" reruns: like I'd be better off dead. It was such a comfort to think that.

But I didn't die.

Hugh Beaumont died.

So long Hugh.

Yes, living is "tricky." What makes it "tricky?"

- I can't have everything I want.
- "Things" won't always be my way.
- There is injustice. It "ain't" always fair.
- Some people will never understand me.
- I can't please everyone.
- There are "givens" to this world.

> *"God grant me the Serenity*
> *To accept the things I cannot change*
> *The courage to change the things I can*
> *and the wisdom to know the difference."*

One night, while at the treatment center, a top-notch, well-recognized therapist spoke. She told my story. She told how she tried to please a husband that could not be pleased, and how she felt her unhappiness was because of him. "If only he would change," she said. She told us how alone and lost she felt, how her husband's behavior caused her stress-related illness, how she wallowed in self pity, lost control of her moods, feelings and behavior. She ended by asking: "What else could I do?"

Obviously the answer was, what did she choose to do?

Don't preach, beg, enable, lecture, but change myself, my reaction, my behavior. Stop trying to fix their crazy world. Do my program. It was like a light went on. I had allowed myself, with my wife and children, to get crazy. I had isolated myself and others to "fix" things. And then, when that woman spoke at the treatment center, I saw it was so simple, though painful and difficult to do. Let others be responsible for themselves.

Life is—
    varied
    haphazard
    complex
    disorderly
    inconclusive
    clear cut
    unified
    harmonious
    meaningful
We can never—
    know enough
    do enough
    be strong enough
to assure full control of everything we want.

21

I believe all the conflict and confusion from all the problems, and all the problem areas, can be put into three major categories:

- Effective problem solving skills. Feeling like I have the power and the ability, the tools.
- Getting along with other people. Allowing them to fulfill their needs while I fulfill mine.
- Entertaining myself in a positive way with a sense of fun and freedom.

When I am not successfully handling these areas, I wallow and whine. Our Number One psychological problem is probably whining.

We have all had gut-twisting moments, or days, followed by sleepless nights, as we search for the reason and cause of our pain. We have all experienced times when there seems to be nothing, no thing, which seems to make sense, which gives us a reason to continue our existence.

Sometimes we wallow in confusion, in unmet needs, in pain, and look to the future for better days.

I wallowed, I chased, I anticipated my wife's needs. I tried to see problems ahead for her, and even went so far as to cut unpleasant news out of the paper. I did everything except take care of myself. When the cardiologist saw how exhausted I was, he suggested a mild sleeping pill. For a brief time I rediscovered how they make me "feel better." It started to weave, or rather I started to weave it, once again into my life. And then, thank God, my friends came to visit me and when they saw what was happening to me, they helped me see my negative self-defeating choice. Together with my family's encouragement, I put myself in a treatment center.

People in pain want relief. Filled with doubt, filled with fears, real and imaginary, filled with anxiety, the world begins to make less sense, and we become less and less a part of it. We try different behaviors, hoping they will give us a sense of belonging, will make us feel good.

When people find themselves alone and lonely, when

they are having trouble solving problems, and when they are uninvolved, a message of pain is being sent.

The cure, for many of us, is to enter the world of Systematic Suicide.* I, in effect, chose this.

*I am indebted to Sid Simon of the Values Realization Field for the concept of Systematic Suicide and have tried to expand on his creative and imaginative work.

three

Systematic Suicide

Now I warn you, this is kind of a scary concept for some. First and foremost, because I have to really, really, really look at myself, my choices, and my behavior.

Secondly, it is scary for some because it implies the chance to change. People, and I'm first in line, resist change. Some of my fellow "change agents" (i.e. helpers, counselors, social workers, nurses, clergy, doctors) are the most resistant to change.

Probably many people reading this book have at one time or another thought of suicide, had a friend or a relative who committed suicide. I myself, in my less functioning days, tried three times. It was never that I wanted to die, as I look back, it was just that I didn't want to live with the pain and saw no other choice.

Let's look at Systematic Suicide.

This is different than jumping.

This is different than driving into a concrete abutment intentionally, as I once did on one of my really crazy days.

This is different than calculating and taking an overdose of pills, which I also attempted.

This is different than blowing your head off with your favorite shotgun.

This is insidious, pervasive, a notch-by-notch, day-by-day destruction of ourselves as an answer to the pain of living.

Without really knowing it, what we do is begin a lifestyle of Systematic Suicide, the lifestyle whereby our behavior becomes oriented toward the relief of immediate pain, at the future expense of our health and general welfare. To the sufferers, it just doesn't matter what happens in the future, because what we are doing today to relieve the intense pain is better than all of the long years of suffering that we put up with.

We think that without this new-found "freedom" from pain, there would be little or no reason to go on in the present, and if this was true, we would probably kill ourselves anyway. So what does it matter if at some point down the road there may be some things that will happen that will bring more pain and possibly shorten our lives? This demand for immediate pain relief at the expense of our future well-being is why we say and hear "I'll quit tomorrow" and why some of us have said, or say, "just one more and then . . . "

Ah, yes, tomorrow. Remember that beautiful musical Annie? I came away whistling the title song. It is all about hopes, dreams, that no matter how bad things are or seem to be, the good life, the changes we will make, are right around the corner . . . tomorrow.

I don't know about you, but tomorrow is always better for me than the pain of dealing with today. That's why I've never started a diet on Friday.

Let's look at Systematic Suicide together.

How are you dealing with your life?

There is no "right" or "wrong."

It is just a way to be "clear." It is in the end your life or like Groucho used to say, "You Bet Your Life."

Here is a chart. All of the "behaviors" qualify for my definition of Systematic Suicide. That is, people use or abuse these to get rid of the pain of living—to feel better.

Before you start to work let's look at them together.

> **Alcohol**—between 1/3 and 60% of all the patients in general hospitals are there because of alcohol. It usually is not stated on the hospital chart, but the secondary aspects are: broken bones—falling down drunk or in an auto accident while drinking; gastrointestinal disorder; heart-related problems; anemia; emotional/psychiatric admissions; malnourishment; burns. Startling, eh? A slow "systematic" death trying to kill pain.

Drugs—I'm not really talking about heroin. There are only about 700,000 heroin addicts in the United States—just about the same number of alcoholics in the city of San Francisco. And I'm not even talking about the widespread cocaine problems. Getting nose operations is becoming one of the leading voluntary surgical procedures. Or even smoking "funny" cigarettes, (isn't it interesting that with all the "pro" and "con" and reams of research and statistical material on marijuana that the key problem is how the marijuana is smoked. It will no doubt cause an epidemic of lung cancer within our younger age group, but that risk is hardly publicized.

The real problem, as I see it, is not the illegal drugs. The real problem is all the millions, yes millions, of people "hooked" on legal, prescribed drugs—the valium to "validate" themselves, the librium to "liberate" themselves, the elavil to "elevate" themselves. We don't need protection from the drug underworld as much as we need protection from the well-meaning physicians. (Two excellent references: *End of a Rainbow* by Mary Ann Crenshaw and *From Chocolate to Morphine* by Andrew Weil, M.D.).

Caffeine—Some say it encourages depression, anxiety, and leads to ulcers. Five cups a day, some say, increases your chances of a heart attack by 50%. Medically, caffeine is classified as a poison. Are you addicted to a poison?

Overeating—Probably our No. 1 addiction is food. Just check the magazine racks for diets—diets—diets—we spend $15-$20 million to lose weight, but the stark fact is that 95% who lose gain it back. Erma Bombeck wrote how she lost 12,740 lbs. since 1948, going on a diet every Monday and has lost the same 20 pounds 637 times. One of the fastest growing self-help groups in the U.S. today is Overeaters Anonymous. When in doubt, when in pain, eat! I'm sure it would be a waste of your time to list the premature causes of death due to overeating. I know them. You know them.

Undereating—The vast numbers of eating disorders and lack of eating disorders are starting to come forward.

Smoking—Can cut our life span by eleven years—our choice.

TV—A one-dimensional technique of not dealing with the world—only sitting and watching—here's the agenda on one of the "Talk Shows" recently:

"Hi there, night owls! Have we got an extravaganza for you tonight! If you're thinking of goin' to sleep, forget it. You won't forgive yourself if you miss . . . the man from the Potato Museum! Later on, you'll meet the guy with the Worm Farm—yes, a colony of live worms to enthrall you tonight! And as if that weren't enough—and you'd better believe it will be—we have an investigative report on . . . Celebrities and their Dry-Cleaning! More Stupid Pet Tricks! An in-depth profile on Alan Alda, the Man and his Chinese Food! And right after this word from one of our several sponsors, we'll place a phone call to Mrs. David Nelson in Loomis, Neb., who's going to tell us all about her social club, the Porkettes, and their Make-It-With-Lard Cherry Pie Bake-Off! I mean, we're gonna have more fun tonight than humans should be allowed to have. But why not folks? Hey?"

TV can become an electronic babysitter or a handy child sedative. People become passive, non-verbal. Studies show the average youngster entering first grade has already spent 5,000 hours "plugged in."

Overspending—One of the leading causes of actual suicide are financial problems. Who feels bad and spends, feels better? Who has "Mastercarditis?" The worry can shorten your life span. Did you know that one of the leading New York Department Stores now gives credit cards to kids 11 and over with their parents' OK? What better way to teach immediate gratification?

Overwork—There are many books now on "workaholics." People using a good cultural ethic (work) to avoid the pain of having to deal with family, love relationships, with living issues because they are always working. Systematically killing themselves but "feeling better" as they do it.

Stress Management and Emotional Management—How well or poorly do I deal with problem solving? Getting along with others? Entertaining myself? How well do I express being mad, glad, sad, angry, scared to be alone? There is much information on what happens to those who "keep it all in," "bite the bullet."

Gambling—Real suicide if you don't pay your debts.

Not Using Seat Belts—That causes those holes in the windshields of cars in the junkyards?

Violence—My pet theory is that people use physical and/or verbal violence to reduce their pain because they don't know any other way to function.

Preventive Medical/Dental Work—Not using the proper medications—not getting checkups—not following advice.

Sexual Addictions—Looking for Mr. or Ms. Goodbar; single bars and single women; hopping into bed when I'm not feeling good, same as seeking any other "high." I believe that Don Juan's issue was perhaps not the conquest of women but the conquest of his own loneliness.

Loneliness—Withdrawing probably has meant eventual and premature death for many— hence people like the Simonton group in Texas use people to combat loneliness in order to combat major illness.

Maybe you could add to the list. Cults? Sleep? Visiting doctors? Too much exercise? Religion? My general definition would be anything that you use to reduce pain and creates or has created problems in your social, family, work life.

After I stopped abusing drugs and alcohol 16 years ago, my primary systematic suicide was 18-hour days of work. I would start at 6 a.m. or 7 a.m. and go until midnight or later. Work, study, overscheduling, never learning to say no. I also have trouble with overeating, not exercising enough, and not taking care of my emotional health. I, at times, choose not to express anger, fear, disappointment. I am overly sensitive and overly needy of approval, love.

Step 1—On a scale of one to ten rank in order how well or poorly you are doing in each category. Ten means not a problem today. One means a serious problem.

Step 2—Pick out some problem areas you would like to work on and put asterisks beside them. It's not necessary to go from ten to one, but maybe from an eight to a five or six. Remember, we strive for progress, not perfection.

Step 3—How much time will you invest in the problem areas you have listed? To A.A., O.A., Weight Watchers, the local gym, jogging, SmokeEnders, etc.

Step 4—How many dollars?

Step 5—I need people. I will speak more of this later on, but list the initials of those people you could use support, validation, help from. Maybe the people who live with you won't smoke around you to help, etc.

Step 6—Finally, I tend to **overcommit** and I want to do everything at once, which usually ends in my doing nothing well. Therefore rank order, in importance, which do you want to tackle first, second, etc.

Well, what did you learn? Relearn? Discover?

One thing most of us learn is the futility of information. Most of us know the harm we are doing, but we keep on hurting ourselves.

How long will you go on hurting yourself?

We find something that feels good, or at least feels better, than what we have been feeling.

We keep seeking that "relief"—
Finally, we are "locked into our behavior"—
We are aware—
Our "intentions" are good—

Finally Step 7—THE Question—**When Will You Do Something?** "Tomorrow," "after the party," "after the holiday," "soon as I finish this carton," "someday," "sometime," "I really should but—". Usually, many people stop here and the consequence is that this has been an "interesting" experience—"I wonder what's next." "Let's move on."

We have the awareness—
We have the intentions—

We choose not to act. We don't want to really, really, **really** want to act. We "want to want to," as we will discuss later.

31

Systematic Suicidal Behaviors

Behavior	Problem ranking*	Problems to work on	Time willing to invest: min. per day/hrs. per week	Willing to invest in correction	Initials of people you want to help you	Rank order of problem
Alcohol						
Drugs						
Caffeine						
Overeating						
Undereating						
Kind of Food						
Smoking						
TV						
Overspending						
Overworking						
Stress Mgt. & Emotional Mgt.						
Gambling						
Not Using Seatbelts						
Lack of Exercise						
Violence						
Preventive Medical/Dental Work						
Sexual Addictions						
Loneliness						

*Problem ranking: If a problem, rank from 1-5 depending on seriousness; from 6-10 if not a problem.

HOW DO I DESTROY ME? LET ME COUNT THE WAYS

"The quickest means by far are guns, a rope,
    and an overdose of dope.
These ways are tried and true, thus I can
    quickly snuff out the candle of life and hope.

The other ways are not as quick as sudden acts,
    but I can destroy myself on the installment plan;
An hour, a day at a time, can be my subtle but
    effective death pact.
It begins when I feel too weary to care and I no
    longer believe I can.

There are pleasant ways, such as smoking and filling
    my lungs with black tars.
To be sure, I could and my voice does rasp, but I can
    always stop before I take my last gasp.
The balm of alcohol does soothe my nerves and
    numb my brain.
    It does help my pain, but what is the gain.
Family fights, lost days, and perhaps in my car a
    sudden crash of flesh and steel.
Then I will no longer feel.

My arteries and waist, bulging with fat from the
    good things I eat—French fries, pizza pies, and
    tasty desserts.
My poor heart pounds so hard to push the blood
    through all my fat, so I find it hard to physically
    exert.
But I eat and diet and diet and eat
    So in my life a thousand pounds to lose is no small
    feat.
My mother's words I hear repeat,
    "Clean your plate, millions have nothing to eat."
The hurts and insults of yesterday I dutifully record
    on the diary of my mind,
Thus I can always recall the time, the day and name of
    someone who was unkind.
The energy I use to keep the diary of my mind
    prevents me from living with joy in the present time.

I have a rendezvous with success. I rush and
    frantically push my body to extreme distress.

These words echo in my mind—compete, compete,
*   and never retreat.*
Strive for the best, so fast my heart does not beat.
Be perfect, no less. Then one day I will have success.
But lost in the din is the voice within crying
*   Stop! Be wise. Is this the life you prize?*
A collection of things gathered while rushing to die
*   but never finding out the "why."*
How do I destroy me? I have counted a few of the ways.
Must I always to destruction flee?
Can't I finally learn to be? To live now with no delay
*   and even learn how to play?*
Where do I begin?
*   By listening to the voice within.*
To decide I want to change and stop the
*   blaming game.*
Then finally I can walk and not be lame.

The price I pay is not cheap
*   but something of value is what I will reap.*
I will begin with hope, reach out with love,
*   Seeking to care and daring to give*
So before I die I will finally live!"

—Author Unknown

What we have been seeing is, you and I with an inability to prioritize—to prioritize time, money, people—LIFE. Over and over and over, seemingly without choice.

"What else can I do?" is the issue.

CHOICE is one answer.

Almost like "the force," "the urge" takes over, and I "go with the flow," so to speak, DESPITE frequently destructive results and ultimate discomfort.

I get angry at myself, angry at others, go to any length to satisfy my feelings of pain, I know "something unusual is happening" yet I "allow" it. Choose it.

What have you done in the last 24 hours to **extend** your life?

To combat your particular Systematic Suicide? To demonstrate Power over yourself?

four

Why Choose Systematic Suicide

Let us now look at the links that keep us together committing Systematic Suicide. What are the factors, and what are some of the qualities that make us more alike than different?

Magical Thinking

It's not a problem. That fourth donut won't show up on my waistline. I won't get lung cancer. My head won't go through the windshield.

You know, I have never met an alcoholic or drug dependent person who, when they were younger, said: "Gee, I'd sure love to be an alcoholic." "Just think, a wonderful life hooked on drugs."

I have done a lot of work with the correctional system and I have never met anyone in jail or prison who said: "Well Lee, I was about 35, nothing to do and decided I'd sure like to do 10 to 15 years in Somers prison."

No, the common phrase is: "It will never happen to me!"

Poor critical thinking ability

Here we see the marketing wonders promising instant items, instant pleasure, instant relief, and the people who buy and use their products and ideas fail to question, challenge, contradict what they are being told.

A lack of positive self worth

We don't feel that we are worth anything so what does it matter what happens to us? More on this later.

An inability to clarify what and who we love

We can't come up with a list of five things we want to do or five people we want to be with. We don't really know what else to do!

An inability to know how to make the future real

When we had little ability to plan for the future, the present made little or no sense. Eat, drink and be merry, for tomorrow we may die—but we don't!

Victor Frankl's works on people in concentration camps, research on prisoners of war camps, the Iranian hostage reports, all indicate the importance of seeing the future as **REAL**. Without this, there is no hope and many "gave up" or "died."

During one of my travels, I met two former Vietnam veterans who had been in a Viet Cong prison camp for five years. Now, I can't imagine what five minutes was like under those conditions. I met them as they were opening a restaurant in Virginia. When I spoke with them, I found out they spent the five years planning that restaurant — they planned the layout, the equipment, the color scheme, the menu — the future was real, and they came through that terror-ridden experience by living "as if there were a tomorrow."

Prisoners in jail talk of "hard time" or "good time," i.e., no future and fighting each day, or doing what you can with courses, trades, groups, activities, and making the most of the situation. Again the future is real, to some.

Little or no belief that we have enough to live for, and what we do have has little worth and meaning to us

We have no sense of how to obtain more than

we now have, other than by an act of "magic" such as as inheritance, winning at the track, or hitting the lottery.

A sense of total inadequacy for solving the everyday problems of living and working

The world feels too big and I feel too inadequate to do more than exist and go along with the direction and dictates of others.

A lack of balance in life's activities

We have an over-involvement and pre-occupation with our Systematic Suicide or thought to the exclusion of having fun, being with a family, working, creating.

A loss of identity as to who we are and what we stand for

My sense of meaning comes from outside of myself.

A sense of abandonment

No one cares, feels, or thinks about who we are or if we exist. The world becomes flat and we become uninvolved with it—except our particular form of Systematic Suicide which in effect we get "involved" with.

No real identification with role models

We have no real relationships with other persons, with personkind, or with a Higher Power as we understand him/her. We have no sense of how what we do affects the rights of others or their right to fulfill their needs in the manner which they choose. In essence, we have no sense of sharing, no sense of accountability, and no meaningful involvement with others.

We have no sense of identification with others whose attitudes, values, and behaviors allow them to cope with everyday problems and to survive in life

We have no sense of control or of our input into creating the "happening" in the present or in the future. Our constant lament is, "things just seem to happen that way." "Why does this always seem to happen to me?" Some people get all of the luck . . ."

We have a faith and a strong belief in miracle solutions for life's problems with the basic belief that the natural consequences of any problem can be "escaped."

We have no sense of control or of our input into creating the "happening" in the present or in the future. Our constant lament is, "things just seem to happen that way." "Why does this always seem to happen to me?" "Some people get all of the luck . . ."

We lack skills of living.

We seem to be unable to relate what we are doing to what we are thinking, to what we are feeling, which is best expressed in terms of a lack of self-control, and a lack of self-assessment. We are bothered by low frustration tolerance, self-deceit, an inability to delay or defray immediate gratification, and a low self-esteem.

We lack interpersonal skills manifested by an inability to relate to others and to build meaningful relationships.

We lack the ability to communicate, to negotiate, to attend, to listen, to empathize, and to share. We have a marked inability to give or to receive love, and to make genuine offers of help.

We are the "victims."

We have an inability to accept the consequences of our behavior and to blame and punish those with whom we are interacting.

We lack critical, judgmental skills in terms of seeking alternatives to our self-destructive behavior. Our world centers in on all which brings immediate relief. This is usually found in sexual activity or within a substance abusing sub-culture. *We simply do not know what else to do!*

My "link" has always been poor self-esteem. No matter what success I have had in business, in counseling, in writing, in lecturing, in relationships, in any of my life, I have never really accepted me as a worthwhile person. It was always, "someday they will catch up with me and find out I am not what they think I am." I ran from myself in my work, by giving, giving, giving. I kept putting out to avoid looking in. Until after the treatment center.

So here we are.

At this point of despair where we are systematically killing ourselves, locked into suffering and pain. This pain can be an opportunity for change and growth. Father Henri Nouwen says it so well when he says that challenges and disappointments are an opportunity to grow. Father Nouwen also notes that mistakes and interruptions are an opportunity to learn.

In order to see how we can change, let's look at the Pathways we went through or are going through to bring change about.

───────── chapter four exercises ─────────

1. Did you do the Systematic Suicide Chart? What **specific** plans and goals do you have, if any? How do you destroy you?
2. What keeps you stuck? Magic thinking? Lack of positive self image? etc.

3. What have you done in the last 24 hours to extend your life?

4. Before we go on to the next chapter, let's redo the Discovery Statements:

I learned that _____

_____

_____

I rediscovered _____

_____

_____

I'm beginning to wonder _____

_____

_____

I was surprised to find that _____

_____

_____

I would like to explore _____

_____

_____

Now, that I think of it, I _____

_____

_____

I would like to follow up on _____

_____

_____

I would like to make a contract with myself to _____

_____

_____

I see the need to ask the support of _____

_____

_____

I want to think more about _____

_____

_____

five

Pathways of Change

As I write this, I am sitting on the balcony of my villa on the sun-filled island of Skiathos in the Aegean. The warmth of the deep blue water welcomes us, as does the ceaseless surf and the miles of sandy beach with deep-hued rocky coves which I stroll almost daily. I am surrounded by thickly-forested, pine-covered mountains. The aromatic herbs and wildflowers drug my nostrils. My small piece of land is covered with olive and fig trees and beautiful purple flowers that bloom all year. At night the sky is filled with brilliant stars, stars so close it seems I can grab a handful.

People are simple here, inscrutably so, and many still make their living in traditional ways. Neither the fish soup nor the music is canned.

Sometimes I am overwhelmed—emotionally—with the beauty of it all. At those times, it is almost impossible for me to believe the days, many years ago, when all I seemed capable of doing was plotting my own demise.

"On the morning of October 15, 1969, in the rooftop restaurant of a Holiday Inn, Lee Silverstein waited for a man with whom he had arranged a business meeting. Lee had arranged many such meetings in his years of wheeling and dealing, but this one was different. This time he was watching for an angel of death, a representative of organized crime. Lee was about to pay $5000 for the privilege of having himself run off the road by professional killers.

Lee stood by a window that gave restaurant patrons a panoramic view of an old, bleak New England city. In the glass, he could see a faint reflection of himself: Thirty-nine years old, shabby,

43

*unshaven, shaking, retching, hungover. He looked
out. It was a long way down. He thought of all the
hotels, all the windows from which he had the
impulse to jump.*

*He had been waiting for death for a long time—
weeks, months, years? His business was going
under. His marriage had long ago sunk into apathy.
Drinking had long since ceased to be fun; he
couldn't even drink enough to get drunk anymore.
Life had become a succession of blackouts. Each day
was the same as every other day: guilt from the night
before, anxiety about the night to come. All that was
left was to have his debts paid and his family provided for. His insurance policy would pay double
indemnity on a murder that was really a suicide
made to look like an accident."*

When I read that passage from *High on Life,* which is the
story of addiction and recovery of myself and two close
friends, my mind is boggled. How could I ever have
chosen, or have come to the point of choosing, death
over life when, since that time, for the most part, I have
savored each day, each hour, each loving contact with
other human beings and times of peaceful solitude.

Here, in the Sporades Islands of Greece, I wonder how I
could have missed the beauty of this world for so long.

I once heard of a child, who, as he heard people
complaining about early death at the funeral of a middle-
aged relative, ask, "Didn't he live a whole life?"

What can I get out of my gift of life?

Do I risk our adventure or stay in the safety of the
crowd?

Do I risk the anger of others as I do this?

Do I challenge "comfort?"

"I had always wondered if . . ."

"I would still like to try . . ."

For so long I did (do you?), as Roberta Flack sings of:
"Pass through the night and miss all the stars."

Joan Kroc, one of the special contributors to the alcoholism field, once gave me a definition of despair: The

saddest lines in world literature were written by Tanaka Katsumi—"I know that my true friend will appear after my death and my sweetheart died before I was born." Do I choose this way of thinking and behaving? Again, the avoidance of *Being* by *Doing*.

six

"I Won't Change"

The first pathway most of us choose when we start looking at ourselves, or being confronted by others, is, **"I Won't Change."**

"Hey, it's really not a problem . . ."

"I don't need your help . . ."

"I can handle it myself . . ."

"Yes, but . . ."

"It just gets out of control once in a while . . ."

"It's not that bad yet . . ."

"If it gets worse I'll do something then . . ."

"I don't want to talk about it . . ."

"Who needs help? **You** need help, not me . . ."

This is the denial stage, when it is unacceptable to admit loss of control over ourselves. Denial can keep us stuck for a long time.

Why? One reason, I think, is that admitting our lives are unmanageable is very threatening.

Also, accepting what I must consider doing is too frightening.

We will do anything, blame anyone ("If you were married to her/him;" "if you had my boss;" "if you had my parents".)

Blame anything—"My father drove over my tricycle when I was three."

"If you had my job." "If you had my problems." "If you had my metabolism." "If you had my past." "I'm an obsessive, compulsive, neurotic, etc., etc., etc."

Blame anyplace—("If you lived in ___ with it's rain, sun, snow, cold, people.")

A member of a fellowship I belong to says that while drinking he found himself often having a series of "bad breaks, misunderstandings, injustices" that led him to hospitals, jails, lost businesses, lost money, lost family.

And, as one of my best friends, Smokey Orcutt, puts it, he would "wind up being in places I didn't want to be, with people I didn't want to be with, doing things I didn't want to do."

Anything, to keep the behavior, which by this time in our life is so familiar, such an old friend, such a love relationship, if you will, that no matter what the consequences, I will find a way to deny and to excuse.

- I "HAVE TO," therefore "I WON'T."
- "It" makes me feel good.
- "It" takes away the conflict and confusion.
- "It" gives me a sense of meaning.
- "It" protects me from being exposed to new experiences.
- "It" protects me from pain, fear, guilt, anxiety, self-doubt.

As in the song Whiskey, Whiskey — "Whiskey, Whiskey, my old friend, I've come to talk with you again, milk of mercy, please be kind, drive this feeling from my mind."

"It" means all this to me, and "You" want me to change? "Get lost!" "Get in the wind!"

The **REAL** problem is—"____ my job, wife, husband, anxiety, background—and on and on."

So long as I can blame, I can justify, I can continue.

This is true be it drugs, alcohol, staying in toxic relationships, nowhere jobs, food.

I do not know of anything that will change me or anyone, in the **"I WON'T"** stage. Sad as it is, people must experience the pain, the consequences, without being rescued or enabled to get to a point of at least looking at their behavior.

About all I can do for someone else is to let them know clearly by my loving, consistent, and predictable behavior, that I will "be there" for them if they decide to look at change.

"They," "We," (I) remain "locked in." We may vaguely want to feel better, and feel that things are not quite as good as they might be.

The "monkeys" are screaming in our heads. But, "I Won't Change."

In actualizing therapy, Everett Shostrum describes the struggle of hope and despair, helplessness and resistance, that points this out:

- "I want more out of life . . . I'm afraid of living it."
- "I want your help . . . but I want to stay in charge."
- "I want your friendship and companionship . . . while I push you away."
- "I want to face reality . . . and find Santa Claus."
- "I want to love . . . I won't open my heart to potential hurt."
- "I want to be close to others . . . leave me alone—I can do it myself."
- "I'm existing . . . but I'm not experiencing anything."
- "I want growth in my work . . . but I won't look at new things to do or new ways to do them."

Meanwhile:

- To me, seemingly small problems and disappointments become major emotional upsets tinged with anger and rage. During my "crisis" I thought some people forgot my birthday. I went "bananas!" PITY POT — PITY POT — PITY POT!

- Seemingly small pleasures of life are no longer satisfying. I have a growing impatience, indifference, and/or boredom, and a demand for a continual succession of gratifying experiences. Being with some of my friends no longer had interest. I was becoming more and more isolated.

- I can't seem to stop thinking about my anxieties and doomful forebodings. For me, I felt doomed in what seemed to be one more disastrous marriage, one more disappointment.

- I'm having difficulty getting along with other people and they with me. Two of my closest friends came to visit me in Greece. I was in such panic about my relationship that I really shortchanged them in terms of time together.

- I am having fear of people and situations that previously never bothered me. I was obsessed with my wife's happiness and in a panic about losing her.

- I am suspicious of people and their motives, especially those displaying sympathy and expressing a desire to help. When my family and friends first suggested treatment, I was convinced that they had a problem, not me.

- I am feeling increasing inadequacy, suffering the tortures of profound self-doubt and unassertiveness.

- I just don't seem to be in charge.

- My days seem to stretch out—pointlessly, aimlessly.

Now, I no longer "won't" change. If only I "could" change, but "I can't." I don't believe that I, or others, really mean this, what we really mean is that, "I want to **want to**—but I can't." I want to want to give up smoking, eating, that relationship, that job, that whatever. "I want to want to, but I can't."

What prevents me? What blocks me? What is it that allows me to accept long-term discomfort and consequences, instead of short-term pain, "locked" into perpetual misery from which there seems no release, no alternative?

Remember, I learned the behavior and feelings because it seemed to bring me more relief from pain than what I had. I was always in pain, "crippled inside" like John Lennon wrote, or as a friend of mine, Jerome Smith says, "looking good — feeling bad."

I don't really want to **know** "other ways" because I "trust" what I have. At least I know what I have now. Yet, like some unfaithful lover, in a slow insidious way, whatever was bringing us relief or joy starts to change.

"It" starts to bring me results I sometimes dislike.

"It" starts to be disappointing—sometimes.

I can't say "It" is always worthwhile.

"It" brings some discomfort, some remorse, some self-criticism, some self-hate, as I seem to now be a prisoner rather than control.

"Maybe one more time."

"I'm sorry."

"Maybe if I move."

"Maybe if I change jobs."

"Maybe if I get a divorce."

I am reminded of the definition of **The Thornbird** from the book by Coleen McCullough.

> "The bird with the thorn in its breast, it follows an immutable law. It is driven, by it knows not what, to impale itself and die singing. At the very instant the thorn enters, there is no awareness in it of the dying to come. It simply sings and sings until it has not the life left to utter another sound. But, we, when we put the thorn in our breast, we know, we understand. And still, we do it."

That's compulsion—doing something despite an awareness of the consequences. "What else can I do?" is the issue. Choice is the factor.

--- chapter six exercises ---

1. When have you said, "I won't change?"
2. What excuses do you use? Who/what do you blame?
3. What do you really, really, REALLY want?
4. Guess what? That's right. Let's do the Discovery Statements again.

I learned that _____

_____

_____

I rediscovered _____

_____

_____

I'm beginning to wonder _____

_____

_____

I was surprised to find that _____

_____

_____

I would like to explore _____

_____

_____

Now, that I think of it, I _____

_____

_____

I would like to follow up on _____

_____

_____

I would like to make a contract with myself to ____

_____

_____

I see the need to ask the support of _____

_____

_____

I want to think more about _____

_____

_____

seven

"I Want to Want to Change—But I Can't"

I believe that there are two prime factors that keep me locked into "wanting to want to." The first is what I call *learned helplessness*. That is, over this long period of time—indeed a lifetime, I have learned to accept helplessness.

Past feelings and past experiences equal a present acceptance, that "I can't." If I believe that I have no control—that control, is "out there," there is no sense in my even trying to change.

In my 20 years of active alcoholism, I tried (I believe), every way known to stop or to gain control. I tried hobbies, vitamins, religion, years of psychotherapy, hospitalizations—so many, euphemistically called GI Series, rather than calling "It" Detoxification—I thought I'd be addicted to Barium, work, no work, a geographic move, change of jobs, drinking only weekends, drinking only every other day, drinking with milk, with aspirin, other drugs, and, no matter what I did, I wound up DRUNK; What was the problem?

A clue to the problem might have been in a prayer that I used to say every morning, while trying to remember what happened the night before and looking to another day of the same craziness. I'd pray, "God, please let me control my drinking." After I did stop, it dawned on me that I never asked God to help me Stop: Just control.

Therefore, I never did really, really, REALLY want to STOP! I "wanted to want to." I wanted to have the pleasure but not deal with the pain of living.

How many of you have tried to diet? How many

ways and times? Smoking? To start exercise? Stop procrastinating? Change your relationship situation? Gain more effective job responsibility? Deal with tardiness? Finish your education?

Yes, I not only learned the destructive answers to my problems, but I learned HELPLESSNESS and HOPELESSNESS. It isn't in "my control".

I believe the second major factor is—*FEAR*. Primarily fear of giving up the things that have worked so well, so effectively for me in the past:

- Denial
- Rationalization
- Blaming self and others
- Projecting failure

and so on. We will look at these together.

From time to time, in my work, women have come to my office. Bruised, battered, sometimes broken bones.

Generally what I ask is, "What would you like to do?".

Generally, they have two answers.

"I want to want to do something, but I'm so afraid that the next person I'm with may even be worse than the person I am with now."

Or, even more poignant, "I want to want to do something, but I'm so afraid to be alone . . ."

There, is the battle for change. No matter what the problem is, the battle is the same. Pain vs. fear: It is only when the pain is great enough that I can start to admit to myself that I have a problem, and only then that I can even start to accept dealing with some of these fears.

Pain can be the opportunity to change. Yet so many well-meaning wives, husbands, parents, friends, professional "helpers," do just the opposite of this basic principle. They help to alleviate the pain, and in doing so "encourage" the person to continue their destructive behavior, for after all, the pain has been lessened, "I've learned this time," etc.

This, "I want to want to" may be, "I don't want to really,

really, **REALLY** put in the effort." The fear of change is too great.

What keeps us blocked?

Let us look closer at the various lessons in learned helplessness and fear that we have acquired over the years—

● **The Tyranny of the "Shoulds"**—"Ought To's" "Musts"—He, She, The World, should, ought to, must be the way I demand it to be otherwise, without control *and* predictability I suffer pain.

I make desires into requirements.

I make desires into demands.

I make desires into absolutes.

Here we feel three main fears:

● **Fear of Rejection:** (I must be loved by all for all that I do.)

● **Fear of Failure:** (Or even greater Fear of Success, what do I do if I succeed?)

● **Fear of Ridicule:** (Others will not approve of what I do), being judged, criticized, blamed or insulted.

Now there is nothing wrong with expectations: To want to be loved; to strive to do my best; not to want inconvenience or distress; to want to feel happy; to not be faced with danger; to have helpful, compassionate friends; to want to overcome a less desirable past history; to not want imperfect solutions; but to accept that it may be the best I can get, and make them work the best they can.

Yes, I "prefer" these things in my life.

Yes, I do not enjoy inconvenience.

But, to be paralyzed, which many of us get because I must have everything and everyone the way I want it, and it must be perfect—well, Good Luck!

Thus, this tyranny is a key factor. My *words* are the key. What I tell myself and what I believe. When I'm depressed ("depressing," "angering," like Glasser suggests), I ask myself, "Who or what are you, Lee, trying to control, and you don't have control?" Or "who or what, is trying to control you, Lee?" Generally, it will immediately lift the feeling.

I'm convinced that a key is to "Let Go." A paradox—I gain control by giving up control.

Instead of "whining" and playing "His Majesty the Baby," if I take control of what I can control, starting with **myself**, then I can achieve heights of happiness and power never imagined.

"LETTING GO"

TO   *let go doesn't mean to stop caring, it means I can't do it for someone else.*

TO   *let go is not to cut myself off, it's the realization that I can't control another.*

TO   *let go is not to enable, but to allow learning from natural consequences.*

TO   *let go is to admit powerlessness, which means the outcome is not in my hands.*

TO   *let go is not to try to change or blame another, I can only change myself.*

TO   *let go is not to care for, but to care about.*

TO   *let go is not to fix, but to be supportive.*

TO   *let go is not to judge, but to allow another to be a human being.*

TO   *let go is not to be in the middle arranging all the outcomes, but to allow others to effect their own outcomes.*

TO   *let go is not to be protective, it is to permit another to face reality.*

TO   *let go is not to deny, but to accept.*

TO   *let go is not to nag, scold, or argue, but to search out my own shortcomings and to correct them.*

TO   *let go is not to adjust everything to my desires, but to take each day as it comes, and to cherish the moment.*

TO   let go is not to criticize or regulate anyone, but to try to
       become whatever dream I can be.
TO   let go is not to regret the past, but to grow and live for
       the future.
TO   let go is to fear less and to love more.

Author Unknown

After four or five days in treatment, I finally decided to let go, let my ego go, let the obsession go. I am here, I told myself, because of my choices. My way hasn't worked this time. I wanted to regain health, so I had to let go, to move on, stop fighting what others might think. I had to let go of Mister Big Shot writer, lecturer, counselor, and let the process and the people take place. Then I felt peace and I was able to begin, again. I began to be open-minded enough to listen and learn.

I am still involved with people and life, but I will not rise or fall because of my lack of control. Out of all the best seller self-help books, and the semi-scientific work on perception and cognitive therapy, Albert Ellis and his irrational beliefs and rational approach, seems to form the basis of most of the best work. He has been, for over 30 years, leading the way. And he gives credit to a Greek years ago who came to the same conclusion, "Men are disturbed not by things, but by the views they take of them," Epictetus 1st Century A.D. "It is not what is happening but what I am telling myself." Not "if only," "if I had . . ."

Therefore, if I want to gain control, I had better start teaching myself a new language:

"Got to/Have " *is* "I choose/I want"

"I can't" *is* "I won't," "I choose not to"

"I must have" *is* "I want," "I would like," "I choose"

"Try" *is* "Choose"

- "It" doesn't do anything to me.
- Everything is the way it "should" be.
- Everyone is fallible.
- It takes two to have a conflict.
- I feel the way I think.

● **An eternal search for "why"** I am the way I am. Some of us have been taught that "elegant insight" will somehow work magic. "If I know why, that will solve my problems." Insight by itself never, ever, ever, ever, made for behavior change. It gives me information, lets me change the answer and think that the feelings will change, instead of realizing, (as many self-help groups in their simplicity saw long ago), that if I change the behavior, the feelings and thinking will follow.

● **THE PAST**—Sometimes I get blocked by believing that whatever happened in the past is the all-important determiner of my present behavior. "I am what I am and will always be this way." Let the past be a guidepost not a hitching post. Bury the dead with the dead. Admit, accept, (not forget, **accept**), move on! The original "cause" is so often lost in antiquity.

● **FEELINGS**—I don't deny feelings, but if I am to move off dead center, I believe I have to act "as if" . . . rather than be paralyzed or wait until I feel better (How long, how long?).

● **LFT**—Albert Ellis' concept of Low Frustration Tolerance. That is the tendency that as soon as "IT," (the pain) starts again, "I can't stand it," "It's awful," "It's horrible," "It's terrible" and I quickly find it justifiable to return to my old habits of thinking and doing.

● **VULTURES**—This is an outstanding contribution of Sid Simon to the world, discussed in detail in his book *Vultures*, and as I discussed in *Consider The Alternative*. Again, from the past, all those self-condemning beliefs in our own inadequacies. (I've been attacked over and over by my "language vultures" since coming to Greece.) All the "I am's" — "That's me" — "I've always been that way." —"That's my nature." It is so painful to accept that, "Then was Then," or that I might not be all I would want to be, accept that, and "move on." It has been "too long."

Too long that I (and you) have been taught and believed we weren't:

- as cute as our sisters, brothers and cousins
- as smart as anyone else
- as strong as the other kids on the block
- as bright as our classmates
- as talented as the kids in the choir or band
- as lovable as other family members
- as worthwhile as those we associated and competed with
- as funny as our friends
- as acceptable as other members of our peer group
- as popular as the cheerleaders
- as good as anyone else

- **DENYING THAT A CHOICE OF CHOICES (ALTERNATIVES) EXISTS**—There are always choices. Some painful. Some difficult. Sometimes I am faced with two bad choices, but always choices.

- **BLAMING OTHERS FOR MY BEHAVIOR**—It sure is easier than blaming myself or accepting my responsibility.

- **VAGUE IMPERSONAL, UNCONTROLLABLE** —I don't know what "force" it is that makes my car turn into Baskin-Robbins. Those are the same people and "forces" that tied me down on many a bar, and force-fed me alcohol through a funnel. Dunkin' Donuts also sends that force out to me and my daughter Elizabeth. "It," "They made me do it." The group, my boss, my wife, the system and "its pressures"—because I am:

- too tall or too short
- too fat or too skinny
- too strong or too weak
- too talkative or too quiet
- the brilliant scholar or the class dummy

- a boy instead of a girl
- a girl instead of a boy
- the only child or one of too many
- the favorite child or the unwanted one
- the first child or the last
- too pretty or too ugly
- too athletic or non-athletic

What a list! Which ones are blocking you from making change? Which ones give you Fear to face them? Which ones have you learned to "Accept" as part of you, along with the impact—Helplessness.

As I hope you may have gathered, some people:
- may need to keep defending what they do
- don't see any other or sufficient alternatives
- are stuck in situations where they can't seem to get co-operation of others
- have a self-concept that is so poor that they don't feel like they deserve any better
- don't know how to prioritize what is important to them
- fear the unknown—the "loss" the "discomfort" and would rather stay "wanting to want." They just don't want really, really, **REALLY**, want to.

Those who choose to break through the fear and pain must learn to **question, challenge, contradict,** all of the blocks to their change. Who, what, when, why, where is the evidence, what can I choose to believe differently?

This importance is so well pointed out in these two quotes, the source of which I don't really know. They were passed on and I'm grateful for the sharings.

Saul Alinsky (1970) once said, "I believe . . . everyone should be questioning and challenging. If I had to put up a religious symbol the way some people have crucifixes, or Stars of David, my symbol would be the question mark. A question mark is a plowshare turned upside down. It plows your mind so that thoughts and ideas grow."

In a similar vein, Klaus Riegel (1976) says, ". . . It is more important to find out how challenges are recognized and how questions are asked rather than how problems are solved and how answers are given."

chapter seven exercises

1. What situations in your life seem like they will never change, never be different no matter what you do? Make a list. What do you control? What is out of your control? (Do you know the difference?)
2. What are you doing, thinking, feeling about the above?
3. What else can you **CHOOSE** to do? Think? Feel?
4. What fears do you have about change? How can you challenge, question, contradict these fears?
5. Discovery Statements:

I learned that _____

_____

_____

I rediscovered _____

_____

_____

I'm beginning to wonder _____

_____

_____

I was surprised to find that _____

_____

_____

I would like to explore _____

_____

_____

Now, that I think of it, I _____

_____

_____

I would like to follow up on _____

_____

I would like to make a contract with myself to

_____

_____

I see the need to ask the support of _____

_____

_____

I want to think more about _____

_____

_____

eight

Maybe I Can Change

Again, Joan Kroc sent this definition of "Hope".

> *"A basic search of every human being from the cradle to grave is to find at least one other human being before whom he can stand naked, stripped of all pretense and defense, trusting that other person will not hurt him but will accept, love and comfort him, because that other person is thus stripped naked and trusting also."*

That to me is the atmosphere needed to come through the Fear. "A-HA"! **I AM** doing the "elected" suffering. I feel the dissatisfaction, the void, the pain. I see now that I might fill the void or pain in a positive rather than negative way. I make a decision, a dedication, if you will, an acceptance that:

- I can choose
- I am accountable for my success
- I can do differently. I see a possible "way out"
- I can seek positives and avoid negatives
- I can choose peace or conflict
- I can choose to leave fear

Yes, the world does not cause my problems. It is my perception, my belief of what the world is "doing to me," or even capable of doing to me that can cause my problems—It really DEPENDS ON MY RESPONSE, my REACTION. Acceptance of what exists between the extremes of importance and omnipotence on any given issue.

Now, I'm starting to believe in a Power within me—not outside of me. "Mister Whisper" that Dory Previn sings about, keeps the glow of HOPE alive.

I really know what I had to do, but fear kept me afraid to change. But, there is no gain without pain and old tapes still play within me.

MISTER WHISPER

when i am going
'round the bend
i got a wild
imaginary friend
when i am driven up the wall
my old friend
he comes to call

mister whisper's
here again
mister whisper's
here again
he's back
in his apartment
in my head
he's back
in his apartment
like i said

just when life
can't get much worse
he tells me
reassuring things
says i'm the
center of the universe
says i'm as good as
presidents and kings

I want to change, "if only" I could figure out a way of doing "it" which allowed me to escape the natural consequences, or at least, to quit with:

- no risk to myself in terms of making other changes
- no pain
- not having to give up my self-indulgent lifestyle
  Albert Ellis says that the key self-defeating ideas that paralyze us, are the demands that:
- the change would be without discomfort
- the change should have everyone's love and approval
- the change should have guaranteed success
  I and others have added additional conditions:
- the change should happen instantly—magically!
- once the change is in effect, it would solve the problem permanently
- no further changes should have to be made
- a "promise" that after the change is made, I will get back my "good job," my wife, my friends, my lifestyle, my stature, my profession, and anything else I lost through my behavior.

Remember, the battle is between Pain and Fear. How long does it take? It takes as long as it takes. Some of us "learn" slower than others.

I believe I will change, or "give up," or "surrender"—for the same reason that I started doing negative things originally in my life: It started to reduce pain. I will stop, or decide to stop, for that very reason. What a paradox! What a circle! The late, great Harry Chapin always used to close his performances with, "All my life's a circle, sunrise to sunset, seasons come and go again, there never seems to be an end." I look to be relieved of this new pain. I seek relief. I "come to believe," that there must be another way.

I accept that I must give up power to gain power.

I start by starting to accept that one person that I've been running from for so long—myself.

The most common thread that we experience with each other is that, at that point where "surrender" takes place, we see that the natural consequences of our life are linked directly to what we have been doing. Simply stated, I created the misery by doing what seemed to me to be so natural. I finally see that what I am doing has caused what I have become.

Most of us reach a point of pain beyond which we choose not to go. That's the point from which I start to choose a beginning, which involves risks to change.

Fulton Sheen said that modern man sought solutions without a cross. "We want a Christ without his nails. Yet there is no Easter Sunday without Good Friday."

In the words of Clark Moustakas:

> "In times of doubt and conflict there is no other way but to find a way from within . . . Thus the person cannot destroy his real self, even though this might please others and bring a gentler life. No matter how many times he is not affirmed, no matter how many times the faith is broken—something is always there within pushing forward insisting on expression . . . If it weren't for this unique life force we would all become robots—controlled, regulated, attuned to the rules and demands of others . . . In the hours alone it is possible to come to know oneself again, to end the confusion and depression and to begin to live again in a real way from the wisdom of one's senses, and in the process to choose this rather than that. But while the person is struggling to find his way back to life again, to give birth to a new path that comes from within, to restore his spirit and passion for life, he needs strong, unqualified, affirming voices, he needs to avoid rejecting people, tentative people and the "yes-but" people who surround him. Only the totally affirming spontaneous, and unreserved can help him in this struggle and give him the courage and strength to return alone to his thoughts and feelings. Only they can help him to discover what he really wants to do and with whom he can take this journey. Help of this kind does not come through words of praise and approbation, but by the

full presence of real persons and by their respect for solitude and privacy—their willingness to let the person risk the darkness and go within alone."

Father Henri Nouwen speaks of this when he teaches about caring:

WHAT IS CARING?

To care is to give attention with intention. When my own intentions dominate any interest in others, I no longer put myself in their world but simply make them part of my own. To care is the human capacity to listen to the other without asking what advantage that has for me, to reach out a hand without expecting a coin in return, to give without condition and to receive with simple thankfulness. To care is therefore, to become present to the other.

To the degree in which I care, I am with someone, I am part of his or her life and world, I have left my own safe world behind and have become part of the often unknown reality of the other. To the degree in which I pay attention to the other, I am where that person is with his or her worries, joys, fears and hopes.

And those who care for me become present to me. When they listen I know they listen to me, when they speak I know they speak to me, and when they ask questions I know it is for my sake and not for their own. Their presence is a healing presence because they accept me on my own terms and encourage me to take my own life seriously and to trust my own vocation.

I care for one another, then, means to become present to one another so we can share one another's life and carry one another's burdens.

Our tendency is to run away from the present reality or try to change it as soon as possible. We want to cure without daring to care, but it is exactly that attitude which makes us into rulers, controllers and manipulators, and prevents a real human community from taking shape. Cure without care creates impatient people, people who do not want to suffer and share one

another's burdens but desire fast and quick changes.
Cure without care creates distance instead of closeness
and often hostility instead of hospitality. Cure without
care is often offending instead of liberating and therefore not seldom refused by those in need.

(An editorial from the Seminar on Caring;
Concepts by Henri J. M. Nouwen)

And, Father John Powell says: "In the sunset of our lives we
will always be judged by how we have loved."

It is Love that will conquer the Fear. That is why, I believe, so
many self-help groups have been so helpful to so many. They
set the atmosphere in which change can take place, in which
people can feel motivated.

That will conquer Fear. Safety. Comfort. Understanding.
Sharing. Consistency. Predictability. An Open, Unconditional,
Non-Judgmental setting to help motivate those of us who get
"stuck." The true Involvement I wrote of in *Consider The
Alternative.*

"Those who love and are separated can live in suffer-
ing, but it is not despair; they know that love exists."

Albert Camus

- I become aware.
- I see I have choices and the power and freedom
  to act.
- I make a decision to act.
- I am alone, but related.
- I become a "doer" not "done to."
- My life will start to have meaning!
- My life will be vital!

─────────── *chapter eight exercises* ───────────

1. What is lacking in your world to make it more
    "safe"?

2. Who can you ask for help? Where can you find an atmosphere to do this?

3. Discovery Statements:
   I learned that _____

   _____

   I rediscovered _____

   _____

   I'm beginning to wonder _____

   _____

   I was surprised to find that _____

   _____

   I would like to explore _____

   _____

   Now, that I think of it, I _____

   _____

   I would like to follow up on _____

   _____

   I would like to make a contract with myself to ___

   _____

   I see the need to ask the support of _____

   _____

   I want to think more about _____

   _____

   _____

nine

From Systematic Suicide to Systematic Growth
(Wellness Tools)

Finding a welcoming, caring atmosphere, will allow me to move from the Fear, from the resentments of past and present, from self pity to Hope, (that is the "possibility" of something different), to Faith, (a belief in myself, a belief in "the process," a belief in a Higher Power of my choosing), to Trust, (a new-found confidence in myself), to Love, (the appreciation of my uniqueness and the uniquess of the people around me).

What this means is that I can "swap":
- confusion
- loneliness
- self-doubt
- despair
- pain

and live in what Father John Powell calls "our vision of life" which will bring with it:
- acceptance (starting with myself)
- the courage to act despite pain
- a sense of fun
- a sense of freedom (having power to fulfill my needs but not interfering with others)
- a sense of worth

Mostly, I can achieve a freedom from fear, really go beyond fear to welcome, to be open to life and beyond that, to be open to love—not only am I surrendering to give up my negative ways of behaving but I can develop a loyalty to myself.

If I act in faith, it is truly miraculous (that is, miracles are unexplained happenings), what appears and occurs. It was always possible, just that I wasn't open to it.

In order to forgive the past, I can practice and experience love in the here and now. I will "judge" myself and be judged by my acts of love.

For me, the hardest part is to find a program, stay with the program, and admit and discipline myself when I deviate.

I try to review each day. Know what went right. Know what to correct. Know what went "unfinished." I know the "process" works, if I let go.

It's my thinking, that will "get me." When I am:
- despaired
- fearful
- critical
- lonely
- jealous
- confused
- resentful
- filled with self pity and contempt
- angry
- afraid
- "guilting"
- "depressing"

I can **choose,** by what I've discussed in this book, through maintaining a loving open mind:
- hope
- faith
- satisfaction
- self-respect
- peace of mind
- forgiveness
- tolerance
- courage
- joy
- self-confidence
- empathy
- friendship

Now, I don't know how you feel, but these are fine words. (I'm even impressed). I do believe all of this. But, how???

Following directions with real tools, that's how.

Steve Glenn, a beautiful person whose counseling work I admire so much, speaks about the differences between "rehabilitation" and "habilitation." His point, which I think is so powerful, is that most people can't be rehabilitated because they never had good tools for living to start with. Therefore, let's "habilitate" people. Help them find and learn the tools.

It is not enough to STOP what I'm doing. I must DO something different.

—————————— chapter nine exercises ——————————

Discovery Statements:

I learned that _____

_____

_____

I rediscovered that _____

_____

_____

I'm beginning to wonder _____

_____

_____

I was surprised to find that _____

_____

_____

I would like to explore _____

_____

Now, that I think of it, I _____

_____

_____

I would like to follow up on _____

_____

_____

I would like to make a contract with myself to ___

_____

_____

I see the need to ask the support of _____

_____

_____

I want to think more about _____

_____

_____

ten

"The Name of the Game is Change"

Here are tools and thoughts that I know work,
if I work them:

- Eating proper foods.

   * * * *

- Maintaining a healthy weight level.

   * * * *

- Adequate, consistent exercise. Modest expectations. Make it fun.

   * * * *

- "Renewal" time—alone time for prayer, meditation, rest.

   * * * *

- Being a risking "Searcher": Physically, Emotionally, Spiritually, Intellectually.

   * * * *

- Having support groups—people who will unconditionally "be there"—people who will stimulate intellectually—people to have fun and play with—people who I know will give me good advice or just listen.

   * * * *

- Avoiding people who drain me emotionally.

   * * * *

- Recreating energy—(not just recreation)—but re-creating, re-energizing, renewing.

* * * *

- Supporting my values—not "selling out"—ethics, standards, ideals.

* * * *

- Continuous work on my love relationships.

* * * *

- Managing, balancing my time: work, play, family, spiritual, alone time, getting rid of "Time Fritters."

* * * *

- Being a love finder, not a fault finder.

* * * *

- Looking at the world with positive, not negative, eyeballs.

* * * *

- Ridding ourselves of **"Red Pencil Mentality."**

* * * *

- Choosing peace of mind over conflict.

* * * *

- Choosing love rather than fear.

* * * *

- Working to eliminate negative criticism for loving messages.

* * * *

- Being open to change—new experiences.

* * * *

When did you last try a new sport or game, a new hobby or craft?

* * * *

- read a new book

* * * *

- take a new course

* * * *

- try new food

* * * *

- travel to a place you have never been before
  (can usually be very nearby)

* * * *

- make a new friend

* * * *

- re-establish contact with an old friend

* * * *

- have a physical checkup

* * * *

- go to a new religious service

* * * *

- risk sharing those feelings you've been keeping
  frozen

* * * *

- Having a sense of humor about me and this crazy
  world

* * * *

- Enjoying art, theatre, music, beauty

* * * *

- Being free of addictions—it's an "addiction" when it
  controls me or when it affects me, my family, my
  business

* * * *

- Stop pretending not to know what I know I know.

- Using self-help programs.

* * * *

- "One Day At A Time." "Now" is all I have.

* * * *

- "This too shall pass."

* * * *

- Prioritize! "First Things First." Learn Goalsetting. Goals must be: conceivable, believable, controllable, measureable.

* * * *

- Don't become too **H**ungry, **A**ngry, **L**onely, **T**ired **(HALT!)**

* * * *

- Accept what I cannot change.

* * * *

- Say what you mean—mean what you say.

* * * *

- Say "Yes" and "No" clearly.

* * * *

- Remember "No" is an honest admission of self limitation.

* * * *

- Treat yourself with the care you'd like from others. You are worthwhile!

* * * *

- Don't "stifle"—air grievances—don't collect them.

* * * *

- Stop "if only!"

* * * *

- "Easy Does It," but DO IT!

- Reach out to others.

* * * *

- "Why Not?"

* * * *

- An attitude of gratitude—just look around—I'm breathing, touching, feeling, smelling, walking, talking.

* * * *

- Name 10 things you are grateful for.

* * * *

- Avoid the Rodney Dangerfield "Pity Pot"—give yourself respect!

* * * *

- Try the *A 12-Step Program for More Likes and Less Dislikes,* by friend Jon Weinberg, available through CompCare.

  1. This is my problem.
  2. I believe I can have results I like better by following a program.
  3. I agree to follow a program that will give me more like results and less dislike results.
  4. I will carefully study what I say and do which gives me and others like and dislike results.
  5. I will share with at least one other person what I discover in Step 4.
  6. I will say what words and actions I need to change in order to have more like and less dislike results.
  7. I will follow a system to learn and practice more helpful ways to talk and act.
  8. I will list those people in my life who were hurt by some of my past behavior.
  9. I will take whatever action I believe will be most helpful to both them and me.

10. I will **continue** to look at the effects of my words and actions on others and myself and work toward increasing the like and decreasing the dislike behavior.
11. I will continue to follow a program learning from all sources of wisdom, and affirm that every person is worthwhile, capable and everchanging.
12. Liking how I am changing in the program I'll teach other people to find more likes and fewer dislikes.

* * * *

• Read—Read—Read—be open-minded to new ideas.

* * * *

• "Let Go."

* * * *

• Live in today! Not "how bad it was"—"how bad it will be"—Today.

* * * *

• Don't wait for the day of judgment—each day is a day of judgment.

* * * *

• Remember, our "thinking" is cunning, baffling, and powerful.

* * * *

• Rejoice in taking power over manageability of your life.

* * * *

• Be available to help others (if they want it)—You keep what you have by giving "it" away.

* * * *

• Practice truthfulness (It's so hard to remember all the lies).

* * * *

- Keep "unfinished" business at a minimum.

* * * *

- What's one thing I can do today that will make this better than yesterday?

* * * *

- Make a list: 20 things I want to do before I die—and start doing them—then add to the list.

* * * *

- Accept the consequences of your behavior (responsibility).

* * * *

- Stop judging, criticizing, putting down.

* * * *

- Full commitment—not "if," "but," "try," "unless," "until." Full commitment in **all** our affairs.

* * * *

- Fulfill your needs—respect and don't interfere as others do the same.

* * * *

- Learn to listen. We listen but we don't hear.

* * * *

- Keep it simple.

* * * *

- **Promptly** admit when I'm wrong.

* * * *

- Eternal vigilance—so easy to slip back to old ways.

* * * *

- Use telephone "buddy" therapy system. Share what's good, as well as not so good.

* * * *

- Let go of anger and fear will go.

* * * *

- Ask for Help. Isolation Kills! Reach Out!

* * * *

- Continue to make inventories of yourself to keep growing. Searching and fearless inventories vs. "Selected Version."

* * * *

- You are not alone—anymore—if you choose.

* * * *

- Look on interruptions, setbacks, problems as invita--tions to learning.

* * * *

- Give up Guilt and "Guilting."

* * * *

- The Chinese word for "crisis" means we can choose the opportunity to grow or fear the danger and miss the opportunity.

* * * *

- Remember I am never upset for the reason I think.

* * * *

- I have the power to **perceive** and act differently.

* * * *

- I am not a victim.

* * * *

- Forgiveness is the key to my happiness. Forgiveness of me and others.

* * * *

- I am responsible for what I see, I choose the feelings I

* * * *

experience, and I decide upon the goal I would achieve. Everything that seems to happen to me, I ask for, and receive as I have asked.

* * * *

- Start each day, without yesterday's burdens. "Empty Headed."

* * * *

- Physically embrace people, touch people.

* * * *

- Watch the sunrise, sunset, moon or stars.

* * * *

- Count success—not failure.

* * * *

- Have a sense of productive work.

* * * *

- Keep hope alive—the possibilities, alternatives I have.

* * * *

- I grow from love **not** anger. Stop! Look! Listen! When I start to get angry.

* * * *

- "What am I doing to me?"

* * * *

- "When to hold, when to fold, when to walk away."

* * * *

- "My parents did the best they could—I deserved better—I accept this and move on."

* * * *

- "Self will run riot."

- I am what I choose.

* * * *

- Stop—Examine—Choose!

* * * *

- Be aware—Make decisions—Act!

* * * *

- Prize—Choose—Act!

* * * *

- Take it Easy—Easy does it.

* * * *

- Accept people as "Doing the best they can."

* * * *

- Think of 10 free ways to have fun today.

* * * *

- Think of 10 expensive ways to have fun today.

* * * *

- Think of 10 ways to have fun with people.

* * * *

- I learn from every experience—none are "BAD."

* * * *

- No one "lets me down" unless I choose to allow it.

* * * *

- I appreciate and accept all that I am—and am not.

* * * *

- I will always have power—if I choose to take power
  (and the consequences).

* * * *

- Don't Panic—Act Don't React—Think!
  (Thanks Lorena)

- Remember what Father John Powell says, "Unconditional love energizes," "What a delight it is to live in your heart."

* * * *

- Anne Frank: "I do believe deep within his heart every person is good."

* * * *

- People, Places, Things, just "Are"—how we respond is the key!

* * * *

- What? So what? Now what?

* * * *

- Remember! PROGRESS **not** PERFECTION.

* * * *

- I will stop placing my "survival" or well-being in charge of a relationship, a job, a car, other peoples' opinions.

* * * *

- I will choose love, faith and be conscious when I try to gravitate away from pain. To face the pain—the fear.

* * * *

- I will choose to adopt co-operation, caring, loving, forgiveness rather than my self-indulgence.

* * * *

- I will give up the need to be perfect—and my demand that others or the world be perfect. Life will never be secure and free of problems or imperfections. At a circus in Athens recently I saw one of the world's great jugglers drop a ball and then move on to "try" again. I will make mistakes—correct them if possible, learn and move on.

- I will choose to RISK. Reaching out. Learning. Challenging. A Bobby Kennedy, "Why Not?" concept. What can I do differently? Better?

* * * *

- I will choose love instead of "Getting Even."

* * * *

- I will choose unconditional love not "Pan-Scale Love" (I'll give you this if you do this).

* * * *

- I will start, as the Course in Miracles teaches, with forgiveness of myself and others.

* * * *

- I will remember what Sid Simon teaches—"I am doing the best I can," "Others are doing the best they can." If I could do better I would. Right now. I might change my mind but then and there I'm doing the best I can.

* * * *

- I will be "Courageous" despite fear, to endeavor one more time, have faith one more time, share one more time, show tenderness and understanding one more time.

* * * *

- Focus on what you can have—not what you don't have.

* * * *

- Choose a new vocabulary that doesn't "control you" or put you down, or put others down, or doesn't compare you or judge you or others—and they act in accordance with your new power words.

The key tools for me are:

- The Serenity Prayer
- and, from the text in the *Course in Miracles,* which has been so important to my recovery:

    "I am responsible for what I see. I choose the feelings I experience and I decide on the goal I would achieve. And everything that seems to happen to me, I ask for and receive as I have asked."

* * * *

- I cannot change people. I can only change, and lucky if I can do that, myself.

* * * *

- People, including and especially myself, are always doing the best they can.

* * * *

- I see so clearly now that whatever happens to me, it is never anyone else that will determine my behavior — except me — my thinking, my trusting the "process," my "Letting Go."

* * * *

—————————— chapter ten exercises ——————————

1. Rank order for yourself 10 tools that you know (really, really, **REALLY**) will help.
2. What tools can you commit to incorporate into your life?
3. For the next three days: "I will specifically—"
4. Discovery Statements:

    I learned that _____

    _____

    _____

    I rediscovered _____

I'm beginning to wonder _____

I was surprised to find that _____

I would like to explore _____

Now, what I think of it, I _____

I would like to follow up on _____

I would like to make a contract with myself to _____

I see the need to ask the support of _____

I want to think more about _____

eleven

To Begin, Again

I came to live in Greece some time ago for basically the same reasons that I lived with the Benedictine Brothers of Mt. Saviour years ago—to re-establish my priorities and goals, physically, emotionally, and spiritually.

My specific and immediate reasons were different: A heart attack, a second heart operation—but basically a continuing search for TRUTH ("Satyagraha" I think is the term Mahatma Gandhi coined.)

So many people saw my stay at Mt. Saviour and my move to Greece as though escaping a wreck to "save myself." I saw both decisions simply as attempts to regain a foothold.

As I move through changes, through conflict and confusion, as I struggle with Systematic Suicide and Systematic Growth—only when I am on solid ground can I regain the power to help myself and others.

I need to continue to return to the simplicity of my soul, which liberates me, which gives me the freedom to once again be reborn—to change again—to grow again—to see the failures and the successes in perspective—to rededicate myself.

I chose Mt. Saviour for reasons made clear in *Consider The Alternative*. I chose Greece because I find here too, the Higher Power's magic is at work—no matter what seems to happen in the world, Greece still seems to remain an almost sacred precinct. It is as if the Higher Power protects this world with Zorbas and Athenas who have such strength as people, despite a history of loss and tragedy, such nobility, beauty, compassion, passions, generosity, curiosity, hospitality, simplicity, that I feel like I am in my "Self Help" program on a full time basis which allows me my needed revaluation, redirection.

Tom T. Hall has a song called "I Love." My "Love List" is so long. I rejoice in each experience and reflect constantly on the blessings I have had since the publication of

Consider the Alternative.

It has been seven years and thousands of copies since *Consider the Alternative* was presented to the public. The response from all corners of the world (just recently it was translated into Spanish and is briskly moving through South America) from people from all works of life brings me such pride and joy to know that I (and Linda and Jon) were able, in some small way, to leave our thumbprint on people's lives.

I never really thought I'd write a publishable book, and so the publication of *Consider the Alternative* was a surprise. The response has been beyond imagination. I could not possibly do justice to the wonderful, extraordinary people I met all over the world. I can simply say "Thank You" and tell you how deeply grateful I am that we have touched each other's worlds—for I was as much the student as the teacher in each human encounter. And oh, the vital energy that each encounter provided! Charming. Caring.

Father John Powell uses a quote from *Camelot*—"It only takes a moment to be loved a whole life through." So true. People send me hundreds of responses: butterflies in every form, shape, painted, tapestries, woven, sculpted, poems and songs in response to my writing; new sources of new Gurus; stories of applying the principles successfully: making contacts, keeping "inventories" up to date, working on living journals. People from every walk of life reaching out as I had tried to reach out. How beautiful, how gratifying, how moving.

My Guru list continues to feed me and grows—*The Course In Miracles*, by the grace of Igor and Diane Sikorsky, the writings of Gerald Jampolsky, Richard Bach's *Illusions*, Anne Lindbergh's works, Joseph Heller's *Something Happened*, the new heights of creativity that Sid Simon continues to bring to this world, the recognition more and more of Albert Ellis' contributions through Cognitive Therapy as so basic to growth, the further work of William Glasser, the re-reading and re-reading of Sheldon Kopp, the milestone work of Claudia Black,

Sharon Wegscheider-Cruse and Jacqui Small; that have added whole new dimensions to the world of addictions; the inspirational and monumental work of Scott Peck's *The Road Less Traveled;* great movies such as *Outrageous* and *Tender Mercies* and my "old" list continues to teach me, to help me help myself and others.

Writing a book of this nature has also had a frustrating side. My workshops, my second book, *High on Life,* a few articles—everything was compared to *Consider* and many times found "wanting" by others—and at times by me.

Praised, but ultimately put down for not creating a comparable "event"—like, if you are going to hit 400, don't do it in your rookie season in the majors. The specter of fading out, becoming non-productive.

Some places wanted, indeed asked for—specifically— "new wisdoms." Some wanted only repetition. This would feed my people pleasing, but not always feed Lee. At times it could create a longing to be "more interesting."

Well **this** attempt to share once again was not an attempt to "outdo." I can and only will do my best each time. I learned quite a while ago that trying to outdo myself can be (maybe was) a deadly game.

THE NEED TO WIN

When an Archer is shooting for nothing
He has all his skill
If he shoots for a brass buckle
He is already nervous,
If he shows for a prize of gold
He goes blind
Or sees two targets—
He is out of his mind!
His skill has not changed, but the prize divides him.
He cares.
He thinks more of winning
Than of shooting —
And the need to win
Drains him of power.

by Thomas Merton

The Tyranny of Expectations, will I expect always be with me. I'm still not fully Rationally Therapized, fully Reality Therapized, all my Values haven't been Clarified. Life at times is unmanageable until I retake control of me.

All I continue to do is work with people who are STUCK. Things aren't going as well as they might—or as they want. Just like myself, maybe you, we constantly struggle.

As I learn and relearn these lessons, I remember a reading from Daily Word. "This is a time of beginning again."

"I MAKE THIS DAY A DAY OF BEGINNING AGAIN"

BEGIN AGAIN—There are times when circumstances change, when human relations change; things we have taken for granted are no longer the same. Such times can be times of consternation if we allow them to be, or they can be times when we trust absolutely in the unchanging care and goodness of God.

We are needed. There are always ways in which we can add interest to our lives. There are always new things to learn, new things to enjoy. There are always opportunities before us to serve and help and bless others.

Rather than looking back and longing for other days, other times, let us say to ourselves, "This is a time of beginning again." Let us make this day and each proceeding day a time of beginning again, a time when we have the courage and the will to go forward in life, expecting new good and trusting God to open new ways to us."

I relearned and learned and will no doubt continue to relearn the need for Eternal Vigilance, for taking care of myself and my program.

The wounds and pains of the past do come alive when least expected. Some days are better than others.

I no doubt will go out of this world like Dylan Thomas' lines:

Do not go gentle into that good night,
Old age should burn and rage at close of day,
Rage, rage, against the dying of the light
Raging to do more, experience more battle the
dragons of the past.

As I said in *High on Life,* I'm still way ahead of where I was—I win more battles with self and life than I lose. I have known what "nothingness" ("no-thingness") means. Sometimes that abandoned little child comes back. Bruised and lonely, but still there. I accept the child in me so much better now. Now I deal with the child within, out in the open and I can do battle so much more effectively.

> *"Yet I have learned the pleasures of risking, touching, compassion, non-judgmental love, joy, and enthusiasm, and I will opt for those prizes each time. I have risked the transparency and found a pleasure that is often spiritual. No longer self-absorbed at all times with that craving for approval, I believe that, as Schweitzer put it, human encounters rekindle the inner light, and that, as Mother Theresa tells us, the mistakes of kindness and compassion are so much more fruitful than all the search for magic cures can ever reveal."*
>
> *High On Life*

I was Lee Silverstein, I will be Lee Silverstein to the best of my ability. That's OK. I know my Higher Power loves me, because each day what I go through good or bad, keeps reminding me of what I can and cannot do, if I trust, if I love, if I have faith. The Higher Power loves me "That Much!"

twelve

So What?

As I come to the end of our journey, (or the beginning), there is a message that I feel would be most fitting. It is a story that Father Henri Nouwen told me several years ago and it is always with me. When darkness, when life seems to block me, when I struggle with conflict and confusion, I always turn to the story of "The Mustard Seed."

THE MUSTARD SEED

A tale is told of the Buddha, the Exalted One, the Possessor of the Ten Forces, and of how he taught his doctrines to the woman Kisa Gotami in the time of her overwhelming sorrow. Kisa Gotami, called the Frail One, had a young son who was the sunshine of her day. It came to pass that hardly had he grown big enough to run and play, when he died. So great was the sorrow of Kisa Gotami that she would not accept the boy's death.

Instead, she took to the streets, carrying her dead son on her hip. She went forth from house to house, knocking at each door and demanding: "Give me medicine for my son." People saw that she was mad. They made fun of her and told her: "There is no medicine for the dead." But she acted as if she did not understand, and only went on asking.

Now a certain wise old man saw Kisa Gotami and understood that it was her sorrow for the dead son that had driven her out of her mind. He did not mock her, but instead told her: "Woman, the only one who might know of medicine for your son is the Possessor of the Ten Forces, he who is foremost among men and gods. Go then to the monastery. Go then to him, and ask him about medicine for your son."

Seeing that the wise man spoke the truth, she went with her son on her hip to the monastery in which the

95

Buddha resided. Eagerly, she approached the seat of the Buddhas where the Teacher sat. "I wish to have medicine for my son, Exalted One," she said.

Smiling serenely, the Buddha answered: "It is well that you have come here. This is what you must do. You must go to each house in the city, one by one, and from each you must seek to fetch tiny grains of mustard seed. But not just any house will do. You must only take mustard seeds from those houses in which no one has ever died."

Gotami agreed at once and delightedly set out to re-enter the city. At the first house she knocked and asked, saying: "It is I, Gotami, sent by the Possessor of the Ten Forces. You are to give me tiny grains of mustard seed. This is the medicine I must have for my son." And when they brought her the mustard seed, she added: "Before I take the seed, tell me, is this a house in which no one had died?" "Oh no, Gotami," they answered, "the dead from this house are beyond counting." "Then I must go elsewhere," said Gotami, "The Exalted One was very clear about this. I am to seek out mustard seeds only from those houses which death has not visited."

On she went from one house to the next. But always the same answer. In the entire city there was no house which death had not touched. Finally, she understood why she had been sent on this hopeless mission. She left the city, overcome with her feelings and carried her dead son to the burning-ground. There she gave him up.

Returning to the monastery, she was greeted by the softly smiling Buddha who asked her: "Good Gotami, did you fetch the tiny grains of mustard seed from the house without death, as I told you to?"

And Gotami answered: "Most honored sir, there are no houses where death is not known. All mankind is touched by death. My own dear son is dead. But I see now that whoever is born must die. Everything passes away. There is no medicine for this but acceptance of it. There is no cure but the knowing. My search is over for the mustard seeds. You, O Possessor of the Ten Forces, have given me refuge. Thank you, my Exalted One.

96

You and I search, you and I struggle with the same sense abandonment, despair, loneliness, grief, anger, emotional pain and discomfort, and I believe that I first need to ACCEPT that as life.

Secondly, if we are willing to risk reaching out to one another, to share our "experiences, strength, hope" it will bring us the POWER we need to overcome the pain.

You might even help others. Another paradox—you will keep what you have by giving it away.

Consider the Choice—The Choice is Yours.

As those beautiful songs tell us: "Come in out of the rain—You've been reaching for yourself for such a long, long time," and "Help Me Make it Through the Night— Let the devil take tomorrow, for tonight I need a friend, Yesterday is dead and gone and tomorrow's out of sight . . ."

That we need one another, is a **Fact.**
That we are with one another, is an **occasion.**
That we can be for one another, is a **privilege.**
I thank you for that privilege.

THE THANKS

"You won't say thanks to me
Just as you don't say thanks to your heartbeats
Carving out the face of your life.

But I will say thanks to you
because I know what I owe you.

That thanks is my song."

Yannis Ritsos

QUOTES

Passage from Don Juan in *Tales of Power*

"Everything we do, everything we are rests on our personal power. If we have enough—one word can change the course of our lives. If we don't have enough the most magnificent piece of wisdom can be revealed and not make a damn bit of difference."

* * * *

"In the sunset of our years, we will be judged by how we loved."—*Father John Powell*

* * * *

"Seeking means to have a goal, but finding means to be free . . ."—*Siddhartha by Herman Hesse*

* * * *

"I know I need to learn patience—where can I get a crash course?"—*Ashleigh Brilliant*

* * * *

"It isn't the experience of today that drives us mad. It is the remose for something that happened yesterday and a dread of what tomorrow may disclose.

"Be still, open your heart, let your feelings be — You are not so different from me. We are the same only with another name. If we have each other we shall win life's game."

— *Thomas McNamara*

"The grand essentials to happiness in this life are something to hope for."—*Joseph Addison*

* * * *

"Realities are no more than possibilities."
—*Sheldon Kopp*

* * * *

"Nightmares are somebody's daydreams
Daydreams are somebody's lies
Lies ain't no harder than telling the truth
Truth is the perfect disguise."
— *Kris Kristofferson*

* * * *

"The key to man's destiny is the ability to reinterpret what cannot be denied."

* * * *

"You are not a carbon copy, you are an original."
—*Father John Powell*

* * * *

"Alcoholism is a diagnosis not an accusation."

* * * *

"The people who know they do not understand each other, breeding children whom they do not understand, and who will never understand them."
—*T.S. Eliot*

* * * *

"The difference between a flower and a weed is a judgment."

* * * *

"Part of forever is better than none."

* * * *

"Attitudes are more important than facts."

* * * *

"Do you want to feel better or get better?"

"Failure is, in a sense, the highway to success, in as much as every discovery of what is false lends to seek earnestly after what is true, and every fresh experience points out some form of error which we shall afterward, carefully avoid."—*Keats*

* * * *

"Whoever gives advice to a headless man is himself in need of advice."—*Sufi*

* * * *

"There's nothing either good or bad but thinking makes it so."—*Hamlet*

* * * *

"A tavern is a day care center with booze."

* * * *

"Begin, the rest is easy."

* * * *

"Many use God only as a giant aspirin. They take Him to avoid pain **only** when they need it."

* * * *

"Don't walk in front of me—I may not follow
Don't walk behind me—I may not lead
Walk beside me—and just be my friend."—*Camus*

* * * *

"A neurotic builds castles in the air;
A psychotic lives in them;
A psychiatrist collects the rent on them."

* * * *

"I think perhaps tomorrow
I'll try to make a friend
To really get
To know him
Instead of pretend
I'll ask him if his feet hurt
Has he burdens to be shared
And if he doesn't walk away
I'll ask him
If he's scared
And if he doesn't walk away
If his eyes don't
Turn to stone
I'll ask him
If he's scared
To be alone."

—*Dory Previn*

* * * *

"Sometimes we hear best the unspoken word—loneliness makes the loudest noise of all."

* * * *

"Freedom is what you do with what's been done to you."
—Sartre

* * * *

"When I repress my emotions my stomach keeps score."

* * * *

"Yesterday's pain may lead to today's understanding and thus to Hope for tomorrow."

* * * *

"I love you in a place
Where there is no space or time
I love you for my life
You're a friend of mine."

— Carole King

* * * *

"Henceforth there shall be
such a oneness
That when one weeps
The other will taste salt."

* * * *

"**G**ood **O**rderly **D**irection."

* * * *

"I pass from interest to interest, but am not satisfied.
Still diseased, twisting, turning, running forward and
  backward in my time.
A bone out of socket. A wanderer in exile."

—*Sam Keen—To a Dancing God*

* * * *

"It is important that we keep breathing
To maintain good health"

—*Lafayette and Indiana Journal*

* * * *

"Faith in Christ is not a matter of creed but of
conduct."

* * * *

103

"Time is too slow for those who wait, too swift for those
who fear, too long for those who grieve, too short for
those who rejoice, but for those who love . . . Time is
eternity."

* * * *

"Each person has one genuine vocation—to find the
way—the task, is to allow life to take its course, to feel
its will and make it MINE."

—Hesse

* * * *

"Act Right, Feel Right!"

—Mowrer

* * * *

"I have had my solutions for a long time
But I do not yet know how I am to arrive at them."

—Karl Frederick

* * * *

"I was in the darkness
I could not see my world
Nor the wishes of my heart.
Then suddenly there was a great light . . .
Let me into the darkness again."

* * * *

"Venture: On an undertaking of chance or danger; the risking of something upon an event which cannot be foreseen with certainty; a hazard."

* * * *

"Keep smiling, it makes people wonder what you've been up to."

* * * *

"Sometimes I go about pitying myself and all the time I am being carried on great winds across the sky."
—*Chippewa Indian*

* * * *

"The flowers of all the tomorrows are in the seeds of today."

* * * *

"Those who bring sunshine to the lives of others cannot keep it from themselves."
—*Sir James Barrie*

* * * *

"Born one foot astride of the grave—we have time to grow old. The air is filled with our cries. But habit is, a great deadener."

— *Waiting for Godot*
—*Beckett*

* * * *

"We are only two and yet our howling
Can encircle the world's end.
Frightened,
You are my only friend
And frightened, we are everyone.
Someone must take a stand.
Coward take this coward's hand."

— *Home of the Brave*
—*Arthur Laurents*

* * * *

"As long as there is love in people's hearts,
Dreams will come true."

* * * *